Voices from Another Place

Voices from Another Place

*A collection of works
from a generation born in Korea
and adopted to other countries*

Edited by Susan Soon-Keum Cox

Yeong & Yeong Book Company
St. Paul, Minnesota

Yeong & Yeong Book Company
1368 Michelle Drive
St. Paul, MN 55123-1459
www.yeongandyeong.com

Book design by Stephanie Billecke

Cover design by John Aeby

Back cover photograph © Ingrid B. Faber

Publisher's Cataloging-in-Publication
(Provided by Quality Books, Inc.)

Voices from another place : a collection of works
        from a generation born in Korea and adopted to
        other countries / edited by Susan Soon-Keum Cox.
        --1st ed.
        p. cm.
        ISBN: 0-9638472-4-4

        1. Adoptees--Literary collections.
        2. Intercountry adoption --Korea--Literary
        collections. 3. Intercountry adoption--United
        States--Literary collections. 4. Korean American
        literature. 5. American literature--Korean
        American authors.   I. Cox, Susan Soon-Keum.

        PS509.A28V65 1999   810.8'0355
                        QBI99-1098

Manufactured in the United States of America

06 05 04 03 02 01 00 99

This book is printed on acid free paper.

to our parents . . .
those who gave birth to us,
and those who raised us.

다함께

다
함
께

Contents

Introduction

SUSAN SOON-KEUM COX

We are a legacy of the destruction of war. In the early 1950s thousands of children—orphaned or left homeless by the Korean war—needed families. Many children did not survive. Some of those who did were adopted into families of other countries. What began as a compassionate response to orphaned children in Korea became a social revolution. Five decades later, intercountry adoption is an accepted global institution.

We were born amid crisis and turmoil, but our lives are a testament of triumph. We are a paradox. Removed from the culture of our birth, we have thoroughly adopted our new cultures. And yet, Korea coats the surface of our skin, is in our bones and speaks to us from the deep past.

The first generation of Korean adoptees were pioneers. Our numbers were small. More often than not, we grew up as the only Koreans in our community. We looked different from everyone around us—including our mothers and fathers. How we fit into our families was a curiosity to others who saw how we looked, but did not understand how we felt. Repeatedly we were asked, "Who are your real mom and dad?"

As the first generation of Korean adoptees became adults, the issues of identity, birth culture, ethnicity and race began to emerge. As we became independent from our adoptive families, established careers, married and had children, many of us also began to long for clarity and to explore our unique citizenship in a global context, to discover and find peace with the balance of our Korean and adopted nationalities.

Many of us have traveled back to our birth country to reconnect with the land we left long ago. Some of us have wondered, inquired or searched for birth families. A few of us have been reunited with them. Increasingly we are reclaiming our Korean names, learning or re-learning to speak Korean and eating *kimchee* with enthusiasm. As we begin or continue on our individual journeys of self-discovery to define who we are, we are also sharing that discovery of identity, heritage and culture with those who now share our lives: husbands, wives, sons, daughters, friends—and the parents who raised us.

Voices from Another Place reflects this first generation of Korean adoptees. It tells our story—we who were first. It exposes the thoughts, feelings and reality of our life experiences. This diverse collection expresses the unique perspectives and personalities of distinct individuals. We are eager to share who we are, tell our stories, encourage and help others by what we have learned or endured. It takes courage to reveal intimate and sometimes painful details of our experiences. There is a great deal of honesty and candor in this book. And there is the unmistakable influence of adoption throughout our lives.

Adoptees are usually identified and defined as children. That we mature, grow up and come into our own wisdom is often not acknowledged. We can and wish to speak for ourselves. The voices in this book all began in Korea. Now these voices speak loudly and clearly and strongly—from wherever they are.

Made in Korea

A Work in Progress

JONATHON KIM HYO SUNG BIDOL

By four in the morning I couldn't wait anymore, but I was too terrified to move. She told me to wait here. I knew she'd be back, but I was worried. Hyo Jung was already asleep at my feet. Her full, round four-year-old face looked placid in the early morning moonlight. Before she finally let go of my hand to fall into the safety of sleep, the combined moisture of sweat and the sticky sweet residue of *dduk* kept us in close contact. Puffy from the smoke and intermittent bouts of crying, her eyes darted back and forth beneath her eyelids. Exhaustion had captured her, but she had me to stand guard.

I kept waiting. She said she would return. "Stay here. Don't move. I'll be back." I was tired and more anxious. It was hard to breathe. The winter air was hot and thick with the smell of burning. My eyes, heavy with sleep, kept crashing closed as I struggled to maintain consciousness and keep from falling on my face. Fifty yards from the factory's flaming front gate, my hunger and the terror of soon-to-be unresolved dreams began to haunt my memory. Nuna had made it clear that I was not to move until she returned. Hyo Jung needed me to stay with her. She said she was coming back soon.

Unprepared for this loss, I have waited twenty-five years. She is waiting for me to say good-bye. While she has never left me, the years of being unable to feel the sorrow and pain have made her memory unreachable. When we were separated that day, I closed my heart and left a piece of myself with that little boy waiting and waiting for my older sister to return.

undertow

ME-K. AHN

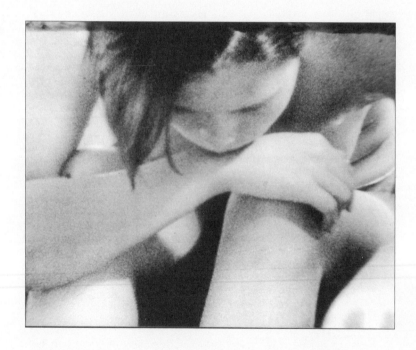

My journey to find my first mother's eyes began when I returned to Korea for the first time in 1992. An endless body of water had suddenly appeared before me, and, like a tiny pebble, my soul fell into the wide expanse, displacing it with a myriad of ever widening ripples. Once it hit the water's surface, I was on my way. I was headed toward an unknown edge, from one life to another. From dusk to day.

I want to see my eyes in my first mother's eyes,
to know where the shape of my legs came from,
the softness of my skin.
A mere glimpse of a photograph may have softened the scars
of my known displacement,
my hidden disconnections.
If I knew where my features came from,
If I knew where I came from,
I could then mend the fissure of body and mind,
of physical geography and cultural landscape.
The figments of a past gone asunder might coalesce
into an unobscured,
even distinct image.

School Daze

THOMAS PARK CLEMENT

Three months after I arrived in the U.S., my father was transferred by his employer from North Carolina to Pittsfield, Massachusetts. Our new home was in a neighborhood near a dairy farm in the Berkshire hills.

I settled into my new home with no apparent problem. Only many years later my mother told me a man who lived several doors away had circulated a petition protesting the introduction of an Amerasian child into the neighborhood. Luckily, he got little support.

I entered first grade at Williams Elementary School without knowing how to speak more than a few words of English. A neighbor, Mrs. van den Honert, saw my plight and volunteered to tutor me in the phonics method of reading. She did this faithfully for several years and I will always remember her kindness.

At school I had a hard time adjusting. When I got frustrated I hid under my desk. My first grade teacher told my parents on Parents' Day, "Little Tommy spends more time under his desk than at his desk." Perhaps I was practicing for air raids. I felt a little more secure with a desk over my head, that's all. Needless to say, I received very poor grades. My first report card contained a steady parade of "U"s (unsatisfactory) with only an occasional "I" (improvement needed). Actually, I blazed a new trail in American education by getting a "U minus" in one instance.

My second grade performance was not much better. Once when we had a math test I copied the paper of a good friend who sat next to me. After the teacher graded the papers she handed them back and said, "Here's a paper for Christopher van den Honert. Very good, Christopher! And here's another paper for Christopher van den Honert. Very good, Christopher! And . . . where is your paper, Tommy?" She knew. I didn't realize what happened until later. I had copied Christopher's whole paper, including his name.

I learned some concepts very quickly though. I learned that it was good to get good grades and it was bad to get bad grades. I learned that when taking a test you are supposed to put your name at the top of the paper, not your friend's name from whom you were copying. Once, when I received a very bad grade on a math test, I went to the boy's room and flushed my bad paper down the toilet. I couldn't bring it home!

When I got back in my seat, the teacher asked me, "Where is your paper, Tommy?"

I had to answer, "I don't know."

She motioned to me with her index finger to follow her. We walked to the little boy's room. There floating in the toilet, because it would not go down, was my very bad test with my name in large letters, "Tommy Clement." I was then escorted down to the principal's office where kindly Miss Coffey gave me a lecture about the school's plumbing system and how expensive it is to fix if broken with my bad papers. Plumbing is a wonderful thing. When it breaks, it's a terrible thing.

Language was the most difficult barrier to my integration into my new wonderful world. I had a lot of trouble expressing my feelings and I didn't know that language was the problem. I had a feeling that it wasn't language, but my limited intelligence. I thought I was stupid.

Birthdays were another strange concept. My mother asked, "What age are you going to be this year?" Because she asked, I thought I got to choose the age I wanted to be. I answered, "I be ten, okay, so I can be same as Carolyn." She burst into laughter.

During my first birthday party when kids brought me presents, I pushed all the presents into a corner to make sure they wouldn't be taken home by the guests. A sense of sharing was not something inherent; it was something I had to learn.

I loved dinner time because everyone in the family sat down together. Our family took turns going around in a circle, each one saying a letter of the alphabet so that I would learn my ABCs. There is a song to help little children learn their ABCs. When it got to be my turn, I said, "LMNO" in one word because in the song, "LMNO" sounded like one letter. The whole family would rock with laughter.

Although I wasn't always well-behaved at dinner, I do remember thinking my brother and sisters sometimes pushed their luck by being unruly. I thought to myself, "This life is good. I am not going to risk being disinvited. I am going to keep a low profile."

There were no other Korean children in Pittsfield that I was aware of, let alone another Korean American adoptee. Though I felt loved by my parents and siblings, I felt most secure spending time alone in fields behind our house. Streams ran through the fields and right across the back of our building lot. My happiest hours were spent catching rainbow and speckled trout with my hands or fishing rod, then dressing and freezing them so that our family could have a trout dinner. My mother showed me how to roll the fish in flour, heat up cooking oil, and cook the fish. They were delicious.

Much of my childhood was spent playing by myself in the woods, making weapons, and hiding them throughout the hills. I made knives from "bandits" lying around construction sites and little huts out of sticks and sod. I was a loner, slow in learning to play with others. I felt better alone with nature because my perceived ignorance was not a factor in the hills and woods. No one was there to pass judgment; there was no "program." I was free to observe nature, the bugs, the animals, the trees, and life itself. I was free and capable.

At times, I had the feeling I was an alien again, a *tuki* (alien devil). Not only because the adoption papers said so, but because, deep down inside, I felt I was. I always kept an eye out for the crash site of my flying saucer. Sometimes I'd stand on a mountain ledge at attention, looking straight ahead. I'd turn my body around in a complete circle as though relaying my whereabouts back to my mother planet. I did this well into my late teens.

My reading rate was very poor; every word was pronounced in my mind as I read. My little sister Leslie had surpassed me in reading speed. She was reading Harlequin novels while I was still laboring through "Puff the Magic Dragon." Sometimes I couldn't even understand what people were saying, so I was often quiet. I was held back in fifth grade because I was doing so poorly academically. The school felt I was not ready to progress to the next grade.

However, I must have impressed someone in school because before I graduated from sixth grade, my teacher took me aside and said, "Tommy, I think you are an exceptionally smart person." I thought he was exceptionally ignorant because I knew how dumb I was.

When I was twelve, my parents received a notification that I was being drafted into the South Korean Army! At that time boys were automatically drafted. In my case a mistake must have been made because I was very young. What my new parents had overlooked was that although I was adopted, I was still a Korean citizen. After much to-do, they obtained my American citizenship. I received a letter from one of the Kennedys congratulating me. It was signed with an original signature. We sent the letter to the Korean Army to prove to them that I was now an untouchable—I was an American.

A War Remembered

SUSAN SOON-KEUM COX

The first time I saw it was from television news reports during the dedication ceremony in Washington, D.C. There was lots of commentary about the "forgotten war" and interviews with men who had been soldiers during that "conflict." Men from Ohio, Kansas, New York, California. They had made the pilgrimage to Washington with wives and families.

The television camera recorded the men standing and gazing reverently at images of soldiers and war on the granite wall of the memorial. They stood quietly before the dramatic larger-than-life-size bronze men, walking in columns, carrying guns and backpacks, with serious expressions on their carved faces. I watched the faces of many of the flesh and blood soldiers become wet with tears. In that moment, I imagined for many of them, they were not standing on the hot sticky grass in Washington, but back in that foreign place forever in their memory.

Music played. Eloquent, noble words were said by important people, and the Korean War veterans standing before the memorial and the thousands of men frozen in time through death were acknowledged.

I watched it all intently, determined not to miss a word or expression. I searched the faces of the men being commemorated. The faces were old. The bronze sculptured soldiers walking in formation through the shrubbery of the memorial were echoes of these men from a much earlier time.

It was not only the soldiers who had died that were frozen in time—for me, all the soldiers of that war remained locked in my memory as they were then. Young, brave, scared. These men were old. They were fathers and grandfathers. They were not the men I remembered.

The war was definitely a part of them. They lived through it. Perhaps scarred, but they endured. Their lives had moved on. They put the war behind them when they left the Land of the Morning Calm.

It should not have surprised me. I did the same. Like these old soldiers, the war is a part of me. I lived through it. Perhaps scarred, but I endured. My life moved on. I put the war behind me when I left the Land of the Morning Calm.

That was four decades ago. One of those men was my father.

For me, it was never a "forgotten war." It was my war. As long as I can remember, I have felt intimately connected to that period in the history of both my birth and adopted nationalities. My father was a soldier of that war. By the time my Korean mother gave birth to me, he was already gone from her life, and from mine. That is the way it is with war. Many casualties, not all of them wearing uniforms. Different kinds of soldiers.

I was birthed by that war.

My father was a soldier, but it was the war that conceived me. Absent that, I would not be. My mother's womb was my incubator, but the root of my umbilical cord was connected not only to my mother, but to the circumstances of the time and place where I would take my first breath of air.

Not a forgotten war.

At the memorial, I run my fingers over the faces of young men etched onto the long granite panels; I remember the faces of the men who stood before these panels. Faces aged and changed by time and years. The two images are incongruent. A kaleidoscope of the past and present blurred together, but still distinct. It is not possible to have only one of the images. They shadow each other.

And so my own life.

My reflection is different too. Aged and changed by time and years. The child I was in Korea during the time of these young soldiers is gone. The soldiers and the little girl, we left Korea. Neither of us chose the war; it took us. The circumstances of the war created me and in many ways shaped my destiny.

I am because of that war. There are times I can trace my deepest, most powerful fears back to those tenuous, shadowy moments that I remember with few specifics and mostly essence. I remember it in my bones and my scared little four-year-old soul.

War terrifies me. It creates in me an intense sense of despair and anxiety that I instinctively connect to fear and sadness and hopelessness—and my own beginnings. War is reckless and insatiable. It feeds on death and destruction. It requires everything, takes everything. I despise everything about war and what it does to people.

But I am here. A living, breathing testimony of incongruency. My life is good. This life birthed by war. I am not a reluctant participant. There are hundreds of thousands of lives like mine that were created by war. There will be millions more.

Standing close to the memorial, I can see myself mirrored on the dark onyx walls amid the sketches of war that are artfully chronicled and preserved. Profiles of soldiers, the enormous gates surrounding the city of Seoul, women in Korean *hanboks,* a few faces of children.

And my own face staring back at me. The bright sun reflects on the shiny black surface. And for a moment, all the images dance and shimmer into one another.

Transition

KEVIN DRAKE

Lim Hwa Sook

LISA DuFORE

To My Daughter's Birth Parents

A Korean Adoptee Writes to the Birth Parents of Her Adopted Korean Daughter

DOTTIE ENRICO

On May 23, 1959, I was admitted to Holt's Nok Bun Dong offices after being abandoned near the City Hall police station in Seoul.

In December 1998, my husband Greg and I traveled to South Korea to adopt our first child—a daughter we named Eleanor Jee Yoon. Before making the trip, we wrote a letter to Eleanor's birth mother in the hope that some day she would return for news of her.

November 2, 1998

To my daughter's birth parents:

I am writing you to let you know that ever since my husband and I learned that we would be adopting your baby, you have been in my heart and in my thoughts. I imagine that this might be a very lonely and painful time for you and that you may be mourning your decision to relinquish your daughter for adoption. I am hoping that this letter will help ease some of the sadness you may be feeling at this moment and provide you with some abiding comfort in the days ahead.

First of all, let me say thank you for the wonderful gift you have given to my husband and me. We have no children, and when we learned that your little girl was about to become a part of our family, we felt a sense of happiness and joy that has made our lives complete. I can tell from her photo that she is a truly beautiful child—such a delicate and serene expression! I imagine that you must be very lovely too, in face and in spirit. Only someone with a good heart and a wise soul could make the kind of sacrifice you are making to insure that your baby is given the best chance for a good life. No parent could be asked to make a more sorrowful choice—the decision to give up a child for adoption. Please believe me when I say that I know how much you love her and that she will always know that you made your decision out of love for her, not out of shame or weakness. Every year, when it is her birthday, you have my sincere promise that our family will think of you and we will remind our little girl that she has birth parents in Korea who are remembering her birthday too.

Before I say any more let me share with you some facts about myself, my husband and our life circumstances. I am not sure how you feel about having your daughter raised somewhere besides Korea. My hope is that you had dreamed that she would be able to grow up in America and that you are pleased.

Because of where we live, your baby will have access to a good education and many cultural opportunities. She will grow up around people from all over the world—Europe, Asia, Africa, Russia—and will learn about their customs, languages and religions. My work has allowed me to meet many famous and interesting people, so she will be exposed to many thoughtful, inspirational men and women. But even though I am going to great lengths to tell you about the educational opportunities and material comforts your daughter will have, please be assured that we will never let her lose sight of life's most important goals—being a kind, loving person, a hard worker and someone who possesses the courage and conviction to battle adversity.

Perhaps the most important thing you should know is that your daughter is also going to be raised in a very special situation because she will be one of only a few Korean adoptees to have an adoptive mother (me) who is also Korean and adopted. Almost forty years ago my birth mother made the same decision you have made and she brought me to Holt so that I could be adopted by an American family. My husband, who is Caucasian and was born in the United States, and I waited a long time to have a child and we could have chosen to have a baby, but we felt very strongly that we wanted to share my experiences as a Korean adoptee with a child who is also Korean by birth, and adopted. I realize this may be very hard for Koreans to understand, but it is not so unusual in America. Adoption is very well accepted in the United States, and I hope this knowledge also brings you some comfort.

Because I will share the special bond of adoption with your child, I believe I will understand what is in her heart and her need to know something about you—her birth parents—in a way that is very personal and profound. If you are wondering whether or not we will teach our daughter about Korea and the Korean people, rest assured that we will. We plan to visit Korea several times while she is growing up, and she will also meet many influential Koreans who live in the United States.

I am sorry if it sounds like I am bragging. I tell you these things in the hope that you will realize that your baby will be loved, cherished and well cared for by her new parents and that she will grow up with people outside of our family who will honor and respect her.

In closing, let me say that if the time comes when our daughter wants to find you or meet you, rest assured that my husband and I will help and support her in her search.

We have yet to meet your baby—our new little daughter—but our hearts are already filled with love for her. I feel particularly close to her since she and I share so much in common—being Korean and being adopted. They say that mothers find a great joy in seeing themselves in their children. Well, even though I will not share the same body and blood as your baby, I will share many of her life experiences, her Korean heritage and her pain over the loss of the parents who gave her life. In that way, you can be sure that you and your memory will always live within each of our hearts and spirits in a very special way.

The Masks We Wear

INGRID B. FABER

A Sense of Loss

MARK FERMI

This is my second trip back from Korea. Each time, I have felt a sense of loss. I thought that going back to Korea would bring me closer to understanding my life better, but it has not. I am going through a sense of loss I do not know or understand, and I keep asking myself why am I feeling this way. My mother asked me, "Why can't you be sad for awhile and understand what it feels like. Life cannot always be happy, you must care for yourself. To do that you must be able to understand and feel all aspects of life." I have come to realize that is true. I have been trying to look at my life in a positive way all the time and not let myself see the sadness and sorrow in my life. My life was built on happy and sad experiences; I need to understand them.

What I feel now that makes me lost and sad I really do not know. I have all these thoughts in my mind but do not let anyone know about them or give myself a chance to understand them because it is too hard and difficult to share. A phrase I go by is: "if I do not know what it is, how can anyone else know and help me?" This phrase stops me from going any further in understanding the difficult things in my life.

Some of the sad experiences I have felt, but never really looked at or written down are: the loss of my birth parents, my birth country and culture, home, someone caring for me, family, love, closeness, happiness, sadness, understanding of my beliefs, honor, pride. A loss of me, a loss of who I am, a loss of what life has to offer me.

Some of these things I have never considered as a loss in my life, but as the way of my life. I can understand them, and it feels like it is no longer a loss. A time to stop wondering and live the life which I wish to live.

Each time I go back to Korea is a learning experience. Each time I return from Korea I am confronted with this sense of loss. It should be all right to feel sad to leave a country and people that I truly love. I no longer need to feel that I will not be able to see Korea or its people. Part of me thought that in Korea I could not find any Korean in me. Korean people asked if I am Korean. I said, "Yes, I am" and question their reaction to my answer. I know I am Korean, although some of my actions do not show it. I can only say a few words in Korean. Just saying "I am not Korean" in Korean makes me feel that way. When I try speaking Korean, I feel I'm not saying it correctly since I repeat it a few times to be understood. Even then, sometimes it does not work. I do not get frustrated, but look at it as a learning experience instead of frustration.

As I look back at my trips to Korea and what they have offered me, I can say the trips have been both great and difficult times in my life. The great times are seeing Korea, its people, my orphanage, new friends, sharing my experiences with others. Difficulties include trying to live my life the same way as before the trips, confronting my personal emotions, not understanding what the trips offer me, trying to understand why people want to help me, sharing my life with others who care about me, and why I can no longer be alone.

I still have a sense of loss and no longer feel I am not moving forward in my life. I've come to realize, from friends who care for and understand me, a sense of what those losses could be. I want to meet my biological parents, but I honor the beliefs I hold that the Korean culture does not allow me to. This conflict keeps me going around in circles. I am afraid to change the culture. Although it may make me happy or sad, that culture will no longer be there. I am not willing to change the culture, but adapt to it. My willingness to understand the culture, my desire to speak and understand the language, makes me both happy and confused at times when I think of them at the same time.

I am afraid of what my biological parents would go through if they met me. How would they be treated by a culture which has a hard time accepting adoption or giving up a son who would carry on the family name. Language would be a barrier between my biological parents and me, preventing us from expressing our feelings without a translator or keeping the communication going after the first meeting.

To understand my sense of loss, I must be willing to do things for me. To look at my beliefs, honor, standards in my life and be willing to change to enable me to be happy. I look more clearly at things that have meaning in my life, willing to risk taking little steps to move forward to better understand what my feelings are.

Part II

This is how I found out I am happy.

I was confronted with issues of Korean culture and birth parents when I came back from Korea last year, and also this year. I have been fighting with those issues for over a year, and finally found peace with them. If I hold what is important now, with the same importance as in the past, then my life becomes confusing. I am trying so hard to keep both, happy within myself. To do that is almost impossible.

Like my unwillingness to give up Korean culture, which is so dear to my heart. Although at times I know the culture can be wrong, that is what I cherish the most now. When I look at my life, I still live in the past regarding the way I see Korea. Mostly I do not want it to change with time; other times I feel differently. It is a heritage I call my own, even though I have not really experienced it. Only what I have read and seen. What I saw on my trip was not the Korea I really wanted to keep in my memories—but those are the memories that are there. I see Korea changing so fast, losing its heritage to a younger generation that does not feel the need to hold on to what is. I guess I am afraid of losing the heritage I remember the most.

Because of my beliefs of Korean heritage, I have given up my decision to really look for my biological parents. That is what keeps me the happiest. I am no longer fighting what I am to do next. I know some day soon, I will start my journey of looking. I am not so overwhelmed that it consumes my life.

That is how I have come to be at peace. I am happy.

I do not feel my life is going backwards anymore. The sense of loss does not feel like a loss—but life.

And Now and Then a White Elephant

Thoughts on the Evening of August 16, 1997

SUNG JIN HALL

After two years of teaching English in China and "finding myself,"
I have come home. So tonight I bake a cake for my mom's birthday. It has been so long since I have made *schwarzwalderkirschtorte*.
I can still remember baking it at Joanna Dreifus's house, to eat
after the high school poetry contest. The cake and my poem—
"Das Karusell," by Rainer Maria Rilke—were both successful; the
cake was polished off and I won first place for my recitation. Nine
years later, all I can remember are a few phrases and the line *"Und
dann und wann ein weisser Elefant."* "And now and then a white elephant." This line appears three times in the poem, serenely and
dependably. Neither then nor now have I made a detailed analysis
of the poem, but it speaks to my condition all the same. Like the
merry-go-round of *"Das Karusell,"* I notice that now and then my
own life has been enhanced by the appearance of elephants.

My birth into Western culture came when I was more than
two and a half years of age. At the Vancouver International
Airport, the only evidence of my identity was a card pinned to
my sweater, printed with my name and the name of the woman
who would become my mom. I did not speak when the entire
extended family met me at the airport. I did not speak during
the ride home in the shiny red Volkswagen bug. I did not speak
that evening as they gave me milk and put me to bed, all without
removing my sweater, "because we were afraid you would cry,"
Mom tells me. I slept and I sweated and I dreamed in sounds
that had so suddenly faded from my ears.

But before the sounds were forgotten completely, I spoke and I taught words to my new mom, and she taught me words of her own. *Kogi,* I said, and pointed. "Meat," Mom replied. *Pap.* Rice. *Bulgogi.* Beef. I liked to eat. I ate everything on my plate and everything my mom gave me, quickly transforming from an undernourished to a sturdy, well-fed girl. I liked other things, too. I liked children and constantly sought out their company. I liked to cut out shapes; paper and my little scissors would keep me content for hours. And I liked to sing. The first song I sang was *"Koggiri,"* a Korean children's song about an elephant. Because I came knowing this song, we call the day I arrived "Elephant Day."

No one and no line of ancestors has provided me with a totem. I have always desired a singular role model, but humans have their limitations. The question keeps haunting me: Can I claim everyone or can I claim no one as my model for living? When I was asking my dad about his stance of conscientious objection during World War II, he said that the question to ask when making important decisions is whether everybody comes out better from certain interactions, essentially the same question that Cummings, Keats, Mencius, and Jesus have responded to with the testimonies of their lives. My dad went on to remind me of his favorite analogy, that "we're all trying to describe the elephant and some of us can describe part of the elephant more correctly . . ." He likes to recite the beginning of the poem: "There were six princes of Serendip, / to learning much inclined, / who went to see an elephant, / though all of them were blind."

I know this story, too, but my version involves mice, not princes. Each of the six blind mice believed in the truth of their experience. The one who felt the tail thought an elephant was like a rope, while the one who felt a leg was sure it was like a column. The mouse who ran up the trunk had faith that an elephant was like a snake, while the one who felt an ear knew the elephant to be like a fan. The mouse who felt the body thought an elephant was like a huge wall. It was only the mouse who ran up and down the length of the whole elephant who could perceive the elephant in its totality.

According to the Chinese zodiac, I was born in the year of the mouse. I am shrewd and intelligent and seldom make long-lasting friends, at least according to what is printed on Chinatown menus. I like to think that the first two predictions are correct, but that the third one is not. What the zodiac animal descriptions do not say is that mice are small and that they are feared by elephants. I don't want to be feared; I don't want my power to come from blind obedience. Neither do I want to accept fear passively. I wish to understand who or what things fear me, and what I fear. The world, like the elephant, can be so huge and overwhelming. Still, the immensity can be comforting when it is nearby, and it can be a beacon when I lose my way. The Chinese character for elephant expresses versatility and honesty. It can function as many parts of speech: a noun, a verb, or a preposition. As a noun it signifies elephant or appearance. As a verb is stands for "be like" or "resemble," and as a preposition "like" or "such as." I am not certain of all that I'm seeking in the elephant, either internally or externally; I am not certain of all that I will or will not find if I choose and name my own totem. But I will continue to look to and to name what is denoted by the Chinese as *da xiang,* the "big elephant," what the Germans call *der Weisser Elefant,* and what I first knew as *koggiri.*

Identity Fugue

JESSICA KOSCHER

Almond eyes . . . olive skin . . . tiny hands and feet . . .
Seem so exotic
All traits . . . sprinkles of my heritage
that equate me

Shame . . . embarrassment . . . discomfiting . . .
I wore my Asian skin in a small white world
becoming numb to the looks and ignorance
surrounding me

Growing . . . evolving . . . transforming . . .
I turned my difference into something powerful
I reveled in my Korean appearance
but remained ignorant . . . in the dark

Embracing . . . expanding . . . maturing . . .
I ponder my heritage
acknowledging my identity fugue
not connecting here or there

I am in the process of awakening
and understanding all that
my almond eyes . . . olive skin . . . tiny hands and feet
mean to my past, present and future

Calling Card (after Adrian Piper)

KATE HERSHISER PARK KUM YOUNG

"Calling Card (after Adrian Piper)" is a business card designed to be a spontaneous empowerment tool. It can be used by any Korean adoptee with limited Korean language skills. The card was inspired by the calling cards of artist Adrian Piper, who used hers as performance props in gender and race dynamics. Kate Hershiser Park Kum Young's ongoing street performance prop was created to actively respond to the demands of the Korean public.

친구에게,

네, 그렇습니다. 영어하고 있습니다. 당신의 반응 때문에 저는 교포라고 말씀드리고 싶습니다. 당신은 잘 모르시겠지만 저는 어렸을 때 입양되어서 외국으로 건너갔습니다. 따라서 우리나라 말을 잘 못합니다. 모국에 돌아온 이유는 한국문화와 한국말을 배우기 위해서입니다. 그래서 당신의 행위로 인해 한국사람들에 대한 편견을 가지고 싶지 않고 당신도 저, 즉 교포들에 대한 선입견을 가지지 않기를 바랍니다. 내가 영어를 써서 당신을 불편하고 언짢게 만들었지만 당신도 마찬가지로 저를 불편하게 만든 것에 대해 유감입니다.

안녕.

Dear Friend,

Yes, I am speaking English. Your comments prompt me to tell you that as you probably guessed I am a kyopo(overseas korean). However, what you probably aren't aware of is I was adopted from Korea when I was young. Consequently, my language skills aren't up to par. My reasons for my return to the motherland are to learn about the culture and language of my own people. Please don't let your behavior be reason for me to stereotype Korean people's attitudes, just as I do not wish for you to have prejudices towards myself, a kyopo. I am sorry if my speaking English offended or threatened your being, just as I am sorry your behavior made me feel uncomfortable.

Sincerely,

Fiber Fashion

KARA JONES

Anything You Like?

Logwood Cloak

A Journey Back

TONYA KEITH

Twenty-seven years ago, two wonderful Christian people made the decision to give a nine-month-old baby girl a chance of a lifetime. My parents already had five birth children: four sons and one daughter. After I arrived, I soon became everyone's baby. My siblings are quite a bit older (the youngest birth child is twelve years older than I am).

As a child, I was a "novelty" in my small country town. We lived close to a large inland military base and many different ethnic military families. I was looked at differently because I had two "white" parents. At age three, I began begging my parents to adopt another little girl so I would have someone to play with. In October of 1976 at the age of four, I got a "big sister." Her name was Sin Yung Sook and she came from Pusan. She was six years old when she came to be part of our big family and became Tamara Danielle Ervin.

Growing up, all of our friends' parents were in their mid-thirties and early forties. Our parents were commonly mistaken to be our grandparents because they were in their fifties. It was depressing at times because they didn't know or care about what was "in style" or they found it difficult to relate to our friends' parents. At other times, it was just embarrassing when we went places and people would comment about their cute granddaughters.

Growing up, my sister Tammy and I always knew we were adopted and it was never an issue of conflict for me. Mom and

Dad always made our adoption papers accessible to us, and we knew the circumstances of our relinquishment, or at least I thought I did. My story was simple. My papers said that my parents were unmarried college graduates. A man, thought to be my birth father, brought me to the orphanage and made the decision for me to be adopted. My parents and I came to our own conclusion as to why I was relinquished. We thought because they were not married it would not be appropriate in Korean tradition to raise a child. We did think it strange that they waited until I was four months old to make the decision. Why didn't they just decide to give me up at birth?

I knew I was loved, had two great parents, awesome brothers and sisters, and a great life. Why would I spend my days wondering about all the reasons why I shouldn't have been given up by my birth parents, with whom I felt no connection and who lived thousands of miles away? It made no sense to me, especially as a teenager who had many more "important" things to think about (dating, colleges, etc.).

In 1990, I graduated with a full academic scholarship and married Rick, my high school sweetheart. Last year, we started thinking about starting a family, and for the first time I began wondering about my biological history. It became important to me to find out about my medical background in case we decided to have children. Although I had always been healthy, it suddenly concerned me to bring a life into this world not knowing anything about my medical background.

Thus, my search began in the spring of 1997. I contacted the adoption agency that placed me, and I completed the necessary applications. For months I heard nothing. I called periodically, to be told that my paperwork and my search was ongoing. One day I received a letter with a document attached that my adoptive parents had never received. The document was called an "Initial Social History," and it contained a lot of information, including my birth parents' names, dates of birth, family history, physical descriptions, and basic medical history.

My husband and I had made the decision a few months prior to participate in the Holt Family Tour in June of 1998. This information brought new meaning to our upcoming trip to Korea. Was I ready after twenty-six years to pursue an even more in-depth search, actually trying to locate my birth parents? After much discussion with my husband and parents, I decided to go ahead, since this was planned to be a once-in-a-lifetime vacation.

So the physical search began to locate one or both of my birth parents. About two weeks before we were to leave, I was notified that my birth father had been located, but it was uncertain if I would be able to meet him on the tour. I was thoroughly disheartened at this point. It's not like one can hop in a car and drive to Korea anytime. I focused on our upcoming trip and my spirits lifted. I tried to put myself in my birth father's shoes and think that he might not want to meet or even correspond with me. He'd had twenty-six years without me; maybe he wanted the rest of his life without Tonya Keith disrupting it.

The day we arrived in Korea I found that my birth father did want to meet me, and it would have to be the following day as he was leaving on a business trip. What a shock! I was not only going to meet him, but it would be much sooner than expected. The rest of the day was a blur. I didn't know exactly how to feel. A part of me was excited to come face to face with someone that I was physically part of, but a bigger part of me was filled with anxiety and uncertain expectations.

I left the group and went back to the hotel so I could change into something less casual. I wanted to show him what he had missed out on all these years in my best attire. As I rode in the cab to the hotel where we would meet, the Korean social worker handed me a letter written by my birth father and pictures of his family. I cannot explain the emotions I felt as I read the letter and viewed the pictures of his wife and children. As I read his explanation of why he had to give me up, I wept. It was a very emotional experience because the reasons that I had believed as I grew up weren't accurate at all. Another difficult fact was that he had two daughters and one son that were younger than I am. It seemed funny because I'm the baby in my family and if I were in his family, I would be the oldest. It was comforting for me when the Korean social worker said he spoke English well. I was very relieved to hear this. In the short time I had been in Korea, I'd already realized what a barrier language could be. Translations from English to Korean were frequently inaccurate.

As I stepped out of the cab in front of the Lotte Hotel, I was completely numb. My legs and arms felt like Jell-O. I was about to meet my birth father for the first time and had no idea what to expect. Coming face to face with him was very strange. We arrived first and sat waiting in the lobby. I remember being very nervous and trying not to have that "deer in the headlights" look as I sat scanning the room for his face. The Korean social worker said, "There he is." I turned to see a distinguished look-ing Korean man with a beautiful woman at his side. He immedi-ately walked toward me and embraced me for what seemed to be an eternity. I stood almost frozen trying to return his hug but barely managing a weak squeeze. He looked me up and down and began to cry. His wife stood silent beside him. He led me to the lobby and we all sat down.

No one said anything. What do you say to the man who gave you up as an infant and now you sit before him as an adult? I was still numb and did not feel anything. I did not cry. He repeatedly commented on how pretty I was and for a few min-utes he and his wife traded words in Korean to one another. He asked the social worker if he could be alone with me, she asked me if it was okay with me, and I said "yes." For some reason, I wasn't afraid of this man I had just met.

When we were alone, he began to recount the story he had written to me in his letter except more candidly and in more detail. He was quick to start by saying that his wife had always known about me and that it was she who had gotten the phone call from the Korean agency trying to locate him for me. He said it was his wife's wish to some day find me again and reunite me with my birth father. My impression of her was that she was very refined, the "traditional" Korean wife. I was astounded that she did everything for him during our meeting (stirring his coffee, sitting silently, walking behind him). I immediately liked her.

My birth father told me in detail the story of his courtship with my birth mother. I immediately asked if he knew where she was because the Korean social worker had been unable to locate her. This seemed odd to me because in Korea, the women keep their maiden names even after marriage. He told me that in the Initial Social History he had not given her name and information correctly so I could never be traced back to her. He said he did this to protect her so she would have a chance at remarriage and a good future. I did not exactly understand this. He went on to say that his mother did not approve of their courtship, but they decided to marry anyway. After I was born, his mother continued to criticize their relationship even more because my birth father had just graduated from college and did not have a job. My birth mother graduated with a degree in modern dance, which his mother did not think was suitable.

When I was three months old my parents separated and my birth mother went to live with her brother. At first I accompanied her, but by Korean tradition children stay with their father, and he came and took me from her. He said it was very difficult taking care of me since at the time I was still nursing, and he said he could never feed me enough. With the pressure of his mother telling him he would never be able to raise a child by himself and because he had no job, he made the painful decision to put me up for adoption. I was now four months old.

Up until this point, I felt sorry for him. Then he told me that he took me down to the Han River and sat on the riverbank and cried before taking me to the orphanage. I was still feeling sorry for him. I asked him how my birth mother took the news. He said he did not consult her and, at the time, she knew nothing about the adoption. Before he said this, I would have been content with the fact that she could not be found and I would never meet her. When I heard him say she had no idea what had happened to her four-month-old baby, I knew then that I had to know her. I had to see her. I had to let her know that I was okay. I let him finish the story. He said that for the next year they continued to see one another secretly. Each time she would ask him, "How is Ji Yung?" He would respond, "She's fine, don't worry." When he knew I had been adopted, he told her the truth. At this time they ceased communication. Who could blame her? Although I do not have children, I cannot imagine the pain and anger she felt toward him.

I wanted to know if he knew where she was, if they had been in contact over the years. He said he knew how to contact her, and periodically they had kept up with one another through a cousin. I was insistent that I wanted to see her while I was in Korea. I would do anything, even if it meant staying longer. He did not feel comfortable with this, for her protection but also for his own selfish reasons. He agreed to try and arrange a meeting for the three of us after he returned from his business trip.

I found myself looking for similarities between us. It was profound how much I looked like him. Later I saw a picture of us with the exact same expression. The more time we spent together, the more I could tell we share some of the same personality characteristics. We are both very headstrong, very opinionated, and detail oriented.

He and his wife took me back to our hotel, and we arranged for him to return the next morning to meet Rick. I couldn't wait to tell Rick all about the meeting and show him pictures of my birth father and his family. I also couldn't wait to call Mom and Dad and tell them what had happened. I'd called them the day before and told them what was happening and they seemed happy for me. I knew deep down they were struggling with this. All my life they were always open and honest with me, but now I was away from them in my motherland, meeting their little girl's biological father. As soon as I told Rick the whole story, I called my parents and told them. I missed my family desperately. My parents seemed happy for me and relieved that I was still "theirs." I knew they were a little insecure, and I think they were even happier that I was still the same Tonya.

The next morning, my birth father and his wife arrived at the hotel to meet my husband for the first time. It was a very formal meeting. Our plan for the day was visiting the Korean Folk Village. My birth father asked if he could join us to spend more time with Rick and me. We toured the village, and my birth father explained everything we encountered. When the time came for us to part, we embraced, and I admit I felt kind of connected to him for the first time. Although I knew we would see each other again soon, I was already missing him a little. This was confusing, and I tried not to think about it. I didn't understand what I was feeling; it was useless to try to sort it out with everything new spinning all around me. I decided I would sort things out when I got home.

Several times during the remainder of our trip away I thought about what my life might have been like had he raised me. It's hard to think about since I don't know him as a person, much less as a father. I must have looked at the pictures of his children a hundred times thinking they were my actual half siblings, yet I felt so unconnected. Another compelling issue was that he did not want to tell them about me yet because he thought they would not respect him the same. To me this seemed selfish, but I didn't really want more siblings. I have six, and that's enough as far as I'm concerned.

The last leg of our tour was fantastic, although my mind was really focused on getting back to Seoul and meeting my birth mother. My birth father called to say that I would be able to meet her. I was ecstatic! Listening to my birth father tell me the story of my relinquishment and knowing she was never informed made me instantly feel connected to her in some way. Feelings of sorrow overwhelmed me. I am not a mother, yet I cannot imagine her grief when he told her a year later he had chosen to put me up for adoption. I wondered why she never insisted on seeing me during that year of separation.

Rick was beginning to understand the role of women and men in Korea, and he kept reminding me that even now women are not equals in a relationship. Twenty-seven years ago it must have been more difficult. The longer we stayed in Korea, the more I believed he was right.

Finally, two days before we left Korea, I came face to face with my mother. She came to our hotel room so we could speak privately. I opened the door and couldn't believe how incredibly beautiful she was. She did not look like she was in her late forties. She was thin, her hair was cut in a chic, short style and she was dressed very western. She came into the room and immediately embraced me and began to cry uncontrollably, whispering she was sorry and she loved me. My heart hurt for her. After what seemed like forever, she calmed down, and we sat next to each other on the couch. My birth father said he wanted me to hear her side of the story, since I had heard his. He promised he would translate her story word for word, that none of her explanation would be compromised. Her story was the same except her feelings toward his mother were harsher, which was to be expected. She brought me a beautiful bracelet and a picture of me taken just before they separated. I was three months old. The picture made me cry. Until then, the only baby picture I had seen was me at nine months in the care of the orphanage. It was really emotional for me.

After she finished telling her side of the story, my birth father took us to dinner. We went to a dinner theater with a Russian magic show complete with Korean ballet dancers. I thought he must have planned this on my mother's behalf since she loved dance; it was what she had studied in college.

As the evening ended, I felt I had come full circle. I felt complete. I finally knew the whole story. I felt no animosity toward anyone. What would be the point? Before I met my biological parents, I didn't feel angry, only uncertainty about not knowing the truth. Knowing "the rest of the story," I felt everything was good in my life. I knew my birth parents felt better too. We had been reunited, and they told me their side of the story in their own words.

I know they will always feel the burden of their decisions concerning me. A little of this burden was lifted the night we met. I feel they will always love each other in their own way, and that brings me inner peace. I know that I was conceived in love, and I understand they each did what they believed was right at that delicate time in both of their lives. Their actions showed me they still care for each other. Both communicated to me privately they would always love each other. My mother seemed like a good-hearted, kind and caring woman. I immediately felt a bond with her and wished we had more time together.

As we prepared to return home, I cannot express the relief I felt. The trip could not have been more educational or more emotional for both Rick and me. I will forever cherish the memories in my heart. Meeting my birth parents is something words cannot explain. It was one of the best experiences of my life. It gave me an appreciation for my upbringing and an understanding of Korean culture that I would have never been able to encounter had I not made the decision to go on the 1998 Family Tour.

Being adopted is special to me. Sharing my story with others is very fulfilling. It gives me greater appreciation for my family, my friends, and my ability to forgive, accept and love others. As my relationship with my birth parents evolves, it brings light to the possibility of growing my family even more. I give credit to my adoptive parents, my "real" parents, for showing me that with your family's love and support, anything is possible in this complicated world.

Hello Good-bye Hello

AMY MEE-RAN DORIN KOBUS

In 1974, at age six, I was adopted into an American family. I still recall my arrival in the United States. I knew something was happening that would change my life forever.

The orphanage *bomo*, my caregiver, woke me before sunrise. It was strange to be awakening so early. The *bomo* had me dress in my only set of clothes, and then she made me brush my teeth. I used an old toothbrush dipped in a bucket of boiled water. My apprehension grew because at the orphanage we rarely brushed our teeth.

In the dimly lit room, everyone was extraordinarily quiet. I could hear the crickets chirping outside, and although a few of the twenty-some orphans pretended to sleep, I knew they were intently watching. Some were propped on their elbows following my movements with silent, wondering eyes. Some of them had seen other orphans go before, never to return. Although I did not know what was going to happen, somehow I sensed that I would not return.

Departing through the outside door, I looked over my shoulder at the other orphans and worriedly smiled at Hyang-sook Lee, my very best friend. She waved, and I saw a tear roll slowly down her cheek. I will remember that moment forever and how, at that time, I did not understand her sadness.

I remember that it was dark and that three Korean women led me along a gravel road. The morning was misty, and we all wore coats to keep out the chill. One woman had a suitcase, and for some odd reason she kept falling down. Maybe the suitcase was heavy. At the end of the road was an old car, waiting. Its lights were bright and stark, piercing the misty darkness. We all climbed into the car.

When we arrived at the adoption office in downtown Seoul, I was brought to the medical examiner's office. Using a stethoscope, a dark-haired man listened to my heart and, to my surprise, gave me painful shots. Then I was shooed into another office where I was given new clothes. I silently put on a white turtleneck, ugly orange-red pants, and a matching jacket with white clovers all over it. I was delighted with the new clothes, but they sure made me itch. I also put on red tennis shoes that had a wide-eyed Korean boy kicking a soccer ball painted on them.

Next I remember being on a huge airplane, escorted by a woman. The engines roared outside my window, and the sky was filled with cotton-like clouds. I still did not understand what was going on, but I was becoming increasingly curious. The plane ride was long, and I slept through most of it. It took more than twelve hours to travel from Seoul to the Twin Cities.

Hello, Minnesota

At the Minneapolis-St. Paul International Airport, my escort took me by the hand and together we walked off the plane into the terminal. I saw a sea of strange-looking people. My escort pushed me toward a group of white people and said in Korean, "This is your new family." She then turned and walked quickly away. Frightened, I spun around and ran back toward her. My new mom picked me up, speaking unintelligible words. I knew no English. While she held me in her arms I kicked, screamed and cried. I pointed outside where another plane was taking off and yelled in Korean that I wanted to go back on that plane. I looked for my escort, but she had disappeared. All the members of my new family surrounded me: my two older brothers, my older sister and my mom and dad. Still kicking and screaming, I was taken to their car.

Everything happened so quickly that it felt as if I was in a whirlwind. My mother pushed me into the family car and held me as I continued to struggle. I was squished between my father and my mother; my brothers and sister eyed me from the back seat. We drove away from the airport, away from everything I knew.

Yet as we drove I became spellbound by the exotic trees and unfamiliar buildings. We drove until it was almost dark. When we finally stopped I was at my new home in North Branch, Minnesota. I was gently taken by the hand to my new house. Someone opened the back door, and as I stood in the doorway a huge black dog leaped on me. The dog seemed bigger than I was, and it barked and licked my face. I was terrified. Later "Charlie" became my very own, and I loved him.

Growing Up "Different"

As I now think about the Korean adoption experience, these memories of my last hours in Korea and first days in the United States are still vivid. My uprooting and transplanting from Korea to America was frightening, yet easy since I had no control over the situation. However, growing up as a Korean adoptee was not so easy. I had more control and lots of time to think of my differences. Small, rural North Branch had only one other Korean resident, also adopted but much older than I was.

In the beginning, I was placed on a pedestal for everyone to look at and adore. I was young, cute, and different. But like most children, my peers soon focused on my physical differences and made fun of them. They were curious about my dark skin, my almond-shaped eyes, and my flat nose. I learned English within a year and forgot my Korean, since I had no one to speak it with. My schoolmates and neighbors made fun of my accent and called me "Chink." They jeered at my Asian eyes. It was painful wanting so desperately to fit in but always knowing that my physical differences hindered my attempts.

I do have some happy childhood memories too. In time a few kids did not care that I was different, and I found a small circle of friends. They appeared to accept me as a child like themselves. I could laugh and play dodge ball just as they could. I could play on the monkey bars and giggle with the others before a film began.

Unfortunately, in all the "fitting in" I denied my ethnic heritage. I learned to dissociate myself from anything Asian. For instance, my family made frequent trips to the Twin Cities to shop and eat at Korean restaurants. At these restaurants, they often urged me to speak in Korean with the Korean waitresses. Usually I would say, "Hi, I'm Amy and I'm American," in English, of course.

I worked diligently to become the model American. I dressed in American clothes, took speech tutoring to rid myself of my Korean accent, and, most important, I acted American. I learned style and behavior from books and magazines and from watching television. I also learned the stereotyped view that Asians are quiet and passive people. So I became outspoken and wild. By many little strategies and tactics I convinced myself daily that I was American—until the next time I looked into the mirror.

The adolescent years were the toughest. Like other teenagers wanting to be popular and accepted by their peers, I would do almost anything not to stand out, not to be different. But the look-alike challenge was greater for me than for my friends. When I finally was allowed to wear makeup, I chose a ghost-white foundation and white face powder in hopes of looking more Caucasian. I must have looked ghastly. Furthermore, like many Koreans, I am petite in height. I tried to be a taller teenager by perming my hair and teasing it up at least three inches above my head. To be American, I had to look American. I tried my darnedest.

Dating was especially difficult. By this time I was in ninth grade, and our family had moved to Superior, Wisconsin. Superior, population 20,000, was much larger than North Branch, yet the residents were fairly homogeneous. Being Korean, I still stood out. When I was allowed to date, at sixteen, I did not have many offers. I think a lot of boys were afraid to ask me out because I was Korean. To them I was not a girl with high grades or good athletic and social skills. I was always "the Korean girl." Boys who dated me would risk ridicule for going with someone supposedly so different.

And I fell in with the racial rules. I internalized them and turned them against myself. For example, even into college, I would date only Caucasian boys. I refused to date Asians. Because I saw myself as less important than whites, to be seen with another Asian would have doubled my shame.

In those years I was not comfortable, nor was I proud to be a Korean. My mom saw my feelings and one day she asked me a penetrating question: "If you can't accept yourself and your ethnic heritage, how can you expect other people to?" I knew right away the question was important. It stuck in my mind, and I often recalled it through my high-school years. But only slowly did I realize its impact and start to grasp its implications. I could never escape being Korean, no matter how American I behaved or how many years of speech tutoring I took or even what makeup I wore. Physically I looked Korean. I remembered my early Korean life. Like it or not, I was Korean. Almost imperceptibly my denial of my heritage started to dissipate. I had always been curious about Korea and in general about Asians.

My mother constantly exposed me and my brothers and sister to my heritage. The summer after I finished third grade, my sister and I attended a Korean school offered in Minneapolis by the Minnesota Language Institute. For several weeks we went to language and culture classes. Through similar experiences, I came in touch with the language, the food, and other adults from Korea. When I had questions about my adoption, my parents readily shared what little they knew of my Korean life. With their constant encouragement to learn more, the curiosity I had hidden since my first day in this country began to spill out.

Yet sometimes it still was difficult to accept my past without knowing more about it. I believe that most adopted children have questions about their biological parents such as, "Why was I given up for adoption?" "Didn't my family want me?" and "Who were my real mother and father?" Those were my questions too. My adoptive parents had little information regarding my biological parents, yet supported my efforts to find the birth family I had lost. As my curiosity grew, my mom told me she had a savings fund that I could use for a trip to Korea after high school. Incredibly—or so it seemed to me—she had been building that fund since the day I was adopted.

A "Motherland Tour"

After graduation, I joined a "Motherland Tour" with twenty other Korean adoptees. We went in search of our biological histories and Korean heritage. I have never been on such an emotional roller coaster.

During the sixteen-hour flight to Seoul I met ten other adoptees about my age. It was strange to be with so many individuals who shared similar non-American roots. We all had many questions to ask yet did not know where to begin. However, once we began talking, we did not stop until we landed in Seoul. We talked about the circumstances that led to our adoptions; we shared concerns about finding our Korean parents.

When we got to Seoul, I was filled with anticipation as well as anxiety. As soon as I entered the airport terminal, my excitement consumed me. I had never seen so many Koreans in one area.

For several days we toured South Korea. After the initial excitement had worn off, I was struck with the realization of how foreign Korea actually was to me. I did not recognize buildings, the language, or the practices of bargaining in the street markets. I felt waves of frustration; for some odd reason, I had expected to recognize my surroundings more than I did.

As we traveled outside Seoul, I marveled at Korea's history. I saw elaborate and still sacred tombs of kings and monasteries from the Shilla dynasty, thirteen centuries ago. I learned that Korea has a rich cultural heritage that can match any country's. The more I saw and learned, the prouder I felt—immensely proud—to be Korean. I visited the Demilitarized Zone (DMZ) near the 38th parallel. I learned the Korean War tore apart hundreds of families, creating numerous orphans like myself. I did not resent the circumstances that led to my being orphaned, but I did resent the misunderstandings between heads of state that often lead to war.

A high point of our tour was eating elaborate meals at Korean restaurants and in private homes. I instantly loved Korean food, which often included sticky rice, savory fish soups and lots of *kimchee*, a spicy Korean dish served at every meal. I was overwhelmed by the variety of dishes served. During these meals, tour members acted like a large family. We often sat at one long table, sharing moments of the day that elicited memories of childhood in Korea.

The nights were particularly memorable. Sometimes we had campfire evenings in the woods where we sang Korean songs and recalled events before our adoption. Our experiences varied. Some were adopted at older ages and remembered a great deal. They recalled their families and the reasons for their adoption. Others were adopted as infants with virtually no memories of Korea. But like me, they still felt a special connection to their motherland.

On our return trip we became temporary escorts, bringing an adopted child from Korea to that child's adoptive American parents. I escorted a thirteen-month-old baby. During the long flight I cared for the baby as if it were my own, knowing I would have to give him up. I thought of my biological mother and her possible feelings when giving me up. I am certain she cried many tears, but was also hopeful and prayed I would be raised by good, loving people. I, too, prayed for the child I held and hoped he was going to a loving family.

The DC-10 finally landed in Detroit. I walked into the terminal carrying the child and holding up a placard with his name written on it. I scanned the terminal until my eyes rested on a similar placard with the baby's adoptive family name. Slowly I walked toward his new family, introduced myself and, a little reluctantly, placed the baby in his new mom's arms. I learned they had adopted another Korean boy about three years before and lived near Detroit. Choked up and holding back a flood of tears, I was unable to talk very much. I wished the family well, exchanged telephone numbers and addresses, and left to catch my connection to Minneapolis.

On the Motherland Tour, I did not find my biological parents. Yet I saw where my orphanage once stood and spent a night at its sister orphanage. The children were adorable. I found myself sad, because they reminded me of my own orphanage experience. I found myself hopeful, because I believed that someday they would be adopted into loving families.

Leaving Korea was tearful but meaningful for our group. I was sad to leave new-found friends who had so much in common with me. We cried over our painful experiences and laughed at some too. Through our stay in Korea, we found and accepted ourselves and most of us arrived at the same conclusion: we are more American than Korean.

Proud to Be Me

At the time I wasn't sure I wanted that conclusion. After all, in seeking out the sights, sounds and feelings of being Korean—in connecting with the Korea in me—I was questioning the culture of my upbringing here. Now, on a Motherland Tour, I discovered the United States was my motherland too. Was I going backward?

Looking back, I would not change being Korean or being adopted. The reasons and circumstances that brought me to the orphanage and adoption are secrets of the past. Every year I learn more about my Korean connection. I no longer live in limbo between two cultures but feel the privilege instead to reap the benefits of the best of both worlds. Moreover, I have strengthened my ties with other minorities to create a support network of African Americans, refugee Asians and people like myself. I finally have realized that as with other people of color, my acceptance in either culture depends on how I see myself, not what others allow me to see.

I am a Korean American adoptee. I am proud to be me.

Perception vs. I Am

TODD D. KWAPISZ

You perceive me as Chinese, Japanese, Vietnamese
    (never mention Korean . . . why?)
You perceive me as the one who started WWII or the
    Vietnam War . . . the Korean War, what was that?
You perceive me as the straight-A student, destroyer of the bell curve.
You perceive me as the model minority myth, the rich person.
You perceive me as the exchange student with my host family.
You perceive me as the Bruce Lees and Jackie Chans . . .
    martial art experts.
You perceive me as a foreigner, until I speak and even then you say
    I speak wonderful English . . . how long have you studied?
You perceive with an identity crisis because my last name
    doesn't match the face.
Your perception is WRONG!

I am Korean American . . . part Land of the Morning Calm and
    part Red, White and Blue.
I am the product of the Korean War which happened between
    1950–1953 ravaging a beautiful country.
I am a student who receives A's only because of hard work.
I am not the model minority myth, but am labeled a minority,
    person of color—a foreigner.
I am with my family who sees beyond race and ethnicity,
    who has both love and courage.

I am a person who owns several black belts only to hold up my
    pants, not to break boards.
I am a person who speaks a language not foreign, but one which
    is natural to me . . . English . . . need some lessons?
I am a person whose last name is correct, even though you
    believe it should be "Lee," "Chang," or "Kim."

What am I?
I am a KOREAN ADOPTEE.
I am an ASIAN AMERICAN.
I am an AMERICAN.
I am an INDIVIDUAL . . .

How to Make a Baby?

MIHEE-NATHALIE LEMOINE

China ink on rice paper

"Baby, you will be
Baby, you will become
the cordon
of the Royal blood
Baby to know
Baby if it has to
the aborted (fetus)
from the fired blood
a life too late
survive too early
from so short . . . laugh
serious . . . I would"

Duotone

KAREN LAIRAMORE PETTY

Time fades
wounds heal
tomorrow is here

East meets West
worlds collide
chances happen

Sun sets
new stars appear
two moons evolve
milky way

Swirling axioms
hazy heaven
gray scales

One hue
picture perfect
duotone

Secrets and Lies

JOY KIM LIEBERTHAL AKA SONG EUN-HEE

they lie to cover up the truth
why lie when the truth hurts just as much?
you know they're hiding
so who are they protecting?
if it's for me, then don't bother
i'll only resent and distrust
so . . . i'll build this wall
so neither lie nor truth
will hurt me
ever.

*(This was written the day after I found out that my birth mother
was looking for me . . . she was never dead, as they told me . . .
I believed them.)*

Who Am I?

KIM MAHER

I look through almond eyes.
I see through rounded sight.
I breathe with set on nose,
And smell the world's delights.

My ears have Eastern shaping.
I hear with Western sound.
My feet touched Buddha's earth,
Then grew on Christian ground.

My lips were shaped for *kimchi*.
My taste seeks hamburger and fries.
I talk with Asian chords.
I speak with English sighs.

My skin is golden yellow.
I feel the pilgrim's part.
I look of Korean parentage.
I love with American heart.

My life, the mixture of many.
The product of different lands.
The sum of nature and nurture.
MYSELF, is who I am.

Never So Distant

HOLLEE McGINNIS

Never so distant
As we may think,

Two hearts entwined
For eternity.

No distance separates
That which is bound

By love, laughter, friendship,
Our relationship profound.

No good-byes for thee
Nor parting sorrow be

An end. Just beginnings
For you held forever in me.

The Stone Parable

JIM MILROY

Growing up in a suburb of St. Paul, Minnesota, during my wonder years was probably just as eventful as growing up in any suburb, with the exception of the number of different races in our household. But we were fortunate enough to escape the sleepy suburban life on weekends by loading into the station wagon and heading up to our family tree farm in Minnesota. Eighty acres of birch and conifer trees growing wild. We knew it was a tree farm because we nailed an official-looking sign on a prominent birch that said "Tree Farm" and my parents' names. Even though the entire eighty acres consisted of nothing but trees, we spent many a weekend planting even more trees. The mandate for tree farms in the sixties was simple. Plant trees. Not to harvest, trim or sell trees. Just plant trees in the land of ten thousand lakes. Watch them grow. Some revolutions are very quiet.

Ironically, my fondest memory of the tree farm is of stones. My brother is just nine months older, and we were never allowed to bring toys to the tree farm. My mother must have thought we'd lose the toys among all the trees. But boys need toys just like tree farms need trees. So we used our imagination. I do not know how it started, but we discovered that we could play cars with stones. It is very likely that my parents told us that during the Depression they were forced to use stones as toys. It worked. My brother and I replaced our Hot Wheels and Matchbox cars with stones. Big quartz rocks became bulldozers.

Long thin skipping stones were Indy racers driven by Mario Andretti. Round shiny rocks became red Corvettes. The most cherished stone? That was reserved for the Bat Mobile. Two brothers playing with stones on a dirt road in rural Minnesota had more cars than Detroit.

My brother has never had to explain to strangers that he is adopted. I have had to explain my adoption all my life. People will believe that stones are cars before they'll accept that my brother, or sisters, or father or mother is my real family. That used to make me very angry until I realized that the mandate for adoption was as simple as the tree farm. Plant families. Not to worry about how others will react or what issues will arise, just plant families. Watch them grow. If they're lucky enough, the rest of the world will see things our way. Some revolutions are very quiet. This one should be written down . . . in stone.

The Rose

KELLY NEFF

My mother sat me down before I left for Korea and asked me to do one simple task. Go to my birth country and "Find her, dolly, please find her."

At first it seemed impossible. My mother wanted me to go to a foreign country where I had no family or friends, a nation that I knew little about, a nation where I did not even speak the language, and find the grave of her daughter—her daughter that she had never carried in her womb, never laid eyes upon, never fed, never sang to, and never held—except in her heart. And nervously wondering if I was going to be able to do this, if I were enough to do this, I told her I would. I would find her.

A long time ago something prompted my parents that they wanted a baby girl. Perhaps it was just a fancy or a whim or a small desire that grew larger and more important and more urgent. They were hopeful, but their second child turned out to be a boy as well. They lovingly cared for their two children, but the desire for a daughter did not leave them.

They decided to look into international adoption. At the adoption agency they were welcomed with open arms. Immediately a child was assigned to them, a small beautiful Korean girl named Lee Kil Soon. My mother cried as she read the letter and looked at the picture of the baby—her daughter.

The next few months were spent in preparation. My brothers could not wait to have a sister. There were baby showers and gifts galore. The nursery awaited the arrival of the new member of the family. Everyone was anxious and happy.

But one day would spoil all of that happiness and crush their hearts and dreams. A letter came saying that their beautiful child in Korea had died from a brain aneurysm. The days that followed must have been hell. Emptiness overtook them as they struggled to continue without their precious girl. Years later, I would look through piles of letters and cards of condolence that my parents received. Yet the one that brought me to tears was from the Social Security office. One stating that since Lee Kil Soon never made it to the United States, she would not receive her American name Kimby May-Lee Neff or her Social Security number. Legally she was not and never was or would be their daughter.

A few days before Kimby died, a baby girl was born somewhere in the city of Taegu, Korea. She, too, was abandoned. That little baby was me. The adoption agency decided that I would be the replacement child for the Neff family. Just like before, a picture and description was sent to the family. My mother, so upset at losing her little Kimby, declared that this new baby was ugly. She did not want this one at all. But as time wore on and more reports arrived from Korea about the tiny child, she decided that she could find room in her heart to take in and love another little girl. I arrived in the States healthy and happy and not nearly as ugly as my mother imagined me to be, and eventually the pain that Lee Kil Soon left in my parents' hearts began to subside.

But it never went away . . .

I arrived in Korea as a part of a Motherland Tour ready to find Kimby—Lee Kil Soon. I was told that Mr. Kim, director of the agency, would spend time with the tour group and knew where the gravesite was. One night, we stayed in my birth city of Taegu. And it was there, in the dark of the subway, that I bought a silk rose. If I found the grave, I thought I could leave it there.

Mr. Kim finally came as promised. He and I set out to find Kimby. The grave was on the other side of the Holt Ilsan Center. No one had been there for years. It had been raining that day, making the air sticky, the ground moist. I looked in the windows of the children's living quarters as we passed by.

There seemed to be three types of children who lived at the orphanage—the ones that got adopted, the ones that didn't, and the ones that never got a chance. And here were all three of them so close together. I, the lucky one, passed by the rooms of those still waiting for families, about to face the one that never got a chance. And the question that had haunted me my whole life arose in my thoughts, screaming, "Why me?"

To get to the grave we passed by the rooms of those children and further still to the edge of the sidewalk and then where there was no sidewalk. We passed on through an overgrown trail and then no trail. We passed under a barbed-wire fence and then up a steep hillside where the Korean vegetation tore at my legs and face. Out of breath and desperately trying to keep up with Mr. Kim, I looked up and saw the gravestone.

The recent rain left the headstone gleaming. I just stood there. On it were hundreds of names of children. Mr. Kim pointed out her name, Lee Kil Soon. I ran my fingers over it. I could not speak or cry. I think that Mr. Kim said a prayer. And then we were off, through the jungle of trees to the Holt Ilsan Welcome Center. It would rain again.

Later in the day, I knew what I had to do. I went back. I brought a small book that Bertha Holt had written and carried with me the rose from the subway. The sun shone triumphantly and this time the children waved and called out as I passed by them. Reaching the edge of the center, I started up toward the grave.

I pulled the weeds around the headstone and let my shoes sink in the red dirt. I found her name again. Placing the book by Grandma Holt on the grave, I carefully rubbed a pencil over her name onto a page. I ran my hand over the wide expanse of the gravestone. Nineteen lines of names by thirteen columns of names tucked far away from society and thought on a Korean hillside. And just me to commemorate them. All of these children were like me, once. Abandoned. And like my birth parents, who will never know if I am still alive, their birth families do not know that they are dead.

And once again I wondered if I was enough. I was the only person in my family to see Kimby's grave. Was I enough to represent the love of a family thousands of miles away? A love so strong that at first they did not want me, the replacement child? Was I enough to stand before this wall of purity and innocence that had been lost? Would I ever be enough to represent them, the children that did not get a voice? That never got a chance?

Sometime while considering this my knees had sunk into the soft, red mud. And my eyes were wet with tears. My hand was clenched around that rose. So small and yellow, from the dark subway, bought and sold, and I thought of them and of me. Tiny children, from humble births, soft, yellow, bought, sold. I placed the rose on the gravestone and watched as the sun beat down on the rose and the stone, screaming with yellow and glowing with love.

Purpose

MEA HAN NELSON-WANG

It is a typical winter day in Seoul, Korea, cold and snowy. I wake up and go to the water pump to get water to boil so I can wash up for the day with warm water. I pump the water and bring it into our kitchen area, where four families share the common space. The kitchen is a flimsily covered area in the corner with a "stove" that's a lump of coal shaped in a circle. Water boils and I go to move the water out of the covered, dark area into some sunlight to wash my face. I step on a piece of ice on the floor and fall. Hot water spills on my right arm. I scream but don't know what to do. My father, hung over from a night of drinking, hears my scream and comes to me to see that my arm is soaked with hot water. I am wearing long sleeved pajamas. He rips open the arm of my pajamas, and we both see the skin from my forearm peeling along with the pajamas. My arm is bloody and steaming. My father, not knowing what to do, gets his bottle of alcohol and pours it over my arm. I scream from the pain and fear.

I lived with my paternal grandmother and father from the time I was four. My parents were never married, but they stayed together for my sake. Finally, when I was four, my mom left my dad because he was an alcoholic and beat her. She left to save her life. She couldn't take me with her because I was the property of my father.

We were very poor, so my family couldn't afford to take me to the hospital or see a doctor for my burn. I remember I was like an invalid; I couldn't move or do anything because my arm hurt so badly. My father and grandmother did what they could.

They tried some home remedies, like spreading butter on my arm. None of it really worked. After several weeks my arm blistered from the water that was absorbed into my skin. I had golf ball sized blisters hanging on my arm for days. At one point, I passed out from the pain. I faintly remember being on my grandmother's back as she carried me to the hospital far away. I was eight and she was in her sixties.

Six months later, I was relinquished for adoption. Burning my arm was the last straw. I was a product out of wedlock, poor, and a girl. Now I had a huge scar. If I had stayed in Korea, my future would have consisted of a marriage to a man with an equally bad scar or defect. I wouldn't be able to get a man on my own with such a condition. My grandmother and father gave me up so I could have a better life than they could give me.

I went to an orphanage where my aunt knew Jane White, the missionary who ran the orphanage. It was actually a children's home and I was too old to be there but she took me in anyway. Because Jane knew my background and family I received special treatment. I stopped going to school while I was in the orphanage, but I got to take piano lessons.

One day when I came back from my piano lesson I went to tell Jane that I had returned. I noticed big shoes outside the door, among many small ones. That was a sign that we had a guest—probably an American. I peeked my head in to say I was back and I noticed the American with a big nose and brown hair. Jane gave him a tour of the orphanage and he played with the children. Months later the same white man with a big nose came back. This time he had his wife with him. She had pretty blue eyes and smiled at me a lot. They took lots of pictures of the orphanage and the children.

Months later, I was awakened very early in the morning and told that I was being adopted and was on my way to America. When I landed in Tucson, Arizona, on October 27, 1979, I saw the same couple. They were now my parents.

My dad's side of the story is that the day when I peeked my head in, Jane said to him, "She needs a good family—like yours!" My dad was in Korea on business and was there to take pictures of the orphanage for my adoptive sister, who had joined the family many years earlier. Prior to his visit, they were thinking of getting another daughter for my sister (they had two biological sons). That same day he called his family in Tucson and told them that he found their new sister. He said that he fell in love with me when I poked my head into the room.

Growing up, people used to ask me about my arm and I hated it. I hated it not only because it was an ugly scar on my arm, but also because it reminded me of a past that I wanted to forget. I didn't want to remember that I was from Korea. I wanted to be American and just fit in. I didn't want constant reminders of what I wanted to forget.

Now, at age thirty, when people ask me about my arm, I am reminded of my life. It gives me a unique history of who I am, why I am here, how far I've come. It has taken me many years of life experiences—tears, anger, frustration, sadness, happiness, love—to understand myself, and to embrace who I am, a Korean American, with a husband without any scars, a loving family, a good career, lots of friends, and an interesting life story.

My mom always said that God had a special purpose for me, that I didn't go through all my experiences in vain. I know what she's talking about now.

It's a Wonderful Life!

JANE OWEN

In large part, I am so far removed from my early years before
adoption and family that it is only a small measure of who I am.
The story of my early years in Korea as a mixed-race "product-
of-war" orphan is largely shrouded in mystery and is— and will
be—forever unknown to me.

Strangely enough, and unlike many of my counterparts, this
knowledge deficit did not and does not disturb me or cause
me great angst. I've often wondered why I am not in emotional and psychological turmoil about birth parents, siblings, the
reason(s) for my being an orphan. The best answer I have is
that the origins of birth and ethnicity only comprise a small
part of "me." That part is primarily physical and genetic. My
slightly Asian features, my naturally curly salt-and-pepper hair,
my small-boned Asian frame (with Caucasian thighs, I might
add) are the "me" that you see. But they are not the essence
of who I am and they do not reflect the process of a shared
history of family.

Family and shared history—maybe these are the key to "me."
I believe my life really began when I was adopted into a group
of people known as a "family." These loving adults and my siblings comprised the beginning of a long and continuous process
which has shaped and molded me into the "me" that I have
become. The me now: wife, mother, grandmother, and nurse
have all been enormously affected by my family of adoption,
not my family of birth.

I now have my own immediate family: three children (two stepchildren and one biological child), and four wonderful grandchildren. Both of my stepdaughters would be uncomfortable (as I would be) for them to be introduced as my stepchildren, because after twenty-five years of being in a blended family, we do not distinguish between biological and step. When rude or overly curious people ask how these two young women can be "my girls," we explain briefly, but otherwise I tell people that I have three children. As for the step-grandchildren, they have no idea that I am anything but their "real" grandmother. My kids call my mother "Grandma."

And so it goes. The cycle and process of being a family is a shared past and a shared future, it is our children and grandchildren. My life started when I was brought into a family to share their past. We now share our future.

I have been to Korea twice since my original "stay" and I am always impressed with the beauty of the countryside, the crowding of the cities and the aggressiveness of the Koreans. They push past you to the elevator or on the subway, and have no qualms about staring at you. I am also somewhat frustrated by the double standard that they hold about Korean-born, now American, adoptees. They want us to be "Korean" by learning the language, eating and enjoying the food, and learning about the customs, and yet they would not keep us as their own and take us into their families to love, nurture, and raise as their own children. They seem to deny that we are Americans by culture, mind set, and family history, primarily because of their rejection of us as orphans. We are only Koreans in appearance.

If my observations about Koreans seem harsh, that is not my intent. I am personally happy to be an American and love my life and am relatively satisfied with who I am. In the words of someone more famous than I, "It makes me proud to be an American!"

Identity

JO RANKIN

Realizing I
Am American first,
Not
Korean. Perhaps
I am
Neither.

Platonic Mother

GREG PYLE

To ask if i Love you is absurd.
To ask if i know you,
that is different.
You know that i do know of you.
You are in my dreams. i am yours,
yet
you are not mine.
i know all that i need
to know when i look in the mirror.
i know all that i care about
when i think of my file.

You left me nothing.
You left me there not knowing who you are.
You left me there with no name,
but you left me with Love.

To ask if i Love you is absurd.
You gave me so little,
Yet so little was too much.
You do not know where
i am, or
where i have been, nay where i'll go, but
i go with you.
You are in my heart, as i am
in yours.
You have my Love.

To ask if i Love you is absurd.
Your Face, i do not know.
Your hands, i have yet to touch.
So many kisses you have missed
so many memories,
You know nothing of.
Your Love i have never heard.
Your Love i have never seen,
and it is your Love i will never
let go of. Yes,
To ask if i Love you is absurd.
i Love you more than you will
never know,
i do not know you.
i do not need to know you
because
i know your Love and it is returned.
Jun, Warg Pyo lives in your heart.
i will always be in your heart, for
you
REIGN
in mine.
i Love you, birth mother.

Full Circle

MELINDA MATTHEWS ROSENTHAL

Forty years ago, a child
Was born across the sea.
She had no past, she had no home,
She had no family.
Her country was in turmoil
And her circumstances grim.
Her soul was strong, her body weak,
Her chance for life looked slim.
But one kind couple far away
Longed for a family,
And chose to love her as she was—
The chosen child was me.

Thirty years ago, a girl
Was growing steadily.
She had a sister—brother, too,
She loved her family.
Her skin and eyes looked different,
And her hair was dark and straight.
Strangers asked her where she slept,
They asked her what she ate.
Sometimes the questions hurt her,
Sometimes, she'd crow with glee,
Most times, she chose to tell the truth—
The questioned girl was me.

Twenty years ago, in school,
A student pledged to be
A true and faithful sister
In a small sorority.
The student felt accepted,
But then the whispers grew—
No other house would want the girl
Not one who looked "like you."
And so the student packed her pride;
She slipped out quietly.
She chose retreat, not battle, then—
The wounded one was me.

Ten years ago, a woman stood
Where once had been a girl.
She'd lived a life of ups and downs,
She thought she knew the world.
She met a man who pledged his love
And so the two were wed.
One son, and then another,
Soon were snuggled in their bed.
The woman's heart was happy,
But more was meant to be.
She chose to love another child—
The chooser now was me.

One year ago, a little girl
Was born across the sea.
She had no past, she had no home,
She had no family.
Her foster family loved her
But they could not keep her long.
She had to find another home,
A place where she belonged.
And then a family far away
Brought her across the sea,
They chose to love her evermore—
My child's come home to me.

Kimchee on White Bread

KARI RUTH

I always hated having my picture taken. How does that old adage go—the camera never lies? I wished it did.

In our family album we have a lot of photos of my hand. Behind it is supposed to be my face. My parents were never quick enough for that reflex of mine. One of the only pics I liked of my actual face is a childhood one of me and my two brothers. Typical Sears purplish-gray swirly backdrop. My older brother is the only one smiling. Big cheesy grin. My younger one looks a little stunned. My pigtail-framed face looks plain pissed. I like it. For a preschooler, it sports some serious attitude.

School picture day was a form of torture for me. I liked getting out of class to wait in line for the photographer. But I always seemed to be back in line on retake day because Mr. Polaroid prima donna snapped the picture just as I blinked. It always seemed to be my fault for the bad original, too, because my eyes squinched up when I smiled. The photographer couldn't tell if my eyes were open or not. I could just not smile or look like I was in a state of complete terror. Either way, my negatives were always a lot prettier.

My high school senior glamour-shot photos look better. But I was still a little disappointed when I got the proofs back. I guess I had imagined that they might airbrush my eyes larger, make my nose a little narrower, my cheeks less round. I thought I might not look so Korean.

I get mistaken for a Korean a lot. A native speaker, that is. As soon as I open my mouth, Koreans are stunned. "But you *look* Korean."

It isn't necessarily my face that Koreans focus on when mistaking me for one of them. It's more my overall appearance.

My Korean friends tell me my style is Korean—my clothes, high-heeled shoes, hair. The makeup isn't the same, but I did start plucking my eyebrows after my first visit to Seoul in the summer of 1997. I was tired of going to the beauty salon and having the stylist try to shave off my attempts to grow a monobrow.

My visiting American friends—also adoptees—sometimes remark on how much I blend in here. Once when I went to meet one, it wasn't until I was right up in her face and said hello that she recognized me. "You look *so* Korean!"

I do like the clothes here. And after living here for 1.5 years, I've accumulated quite a wardrobe.

For the first time in my life, my pants aren't hanging loose in all the wrong places. The crotch isn't at my knees, I don't have extra hip room to fill. Everything is proportional to my body shape. My work suits fit like they are tailor-made. The only thing I don't like are the shirts. Too form-fitting. Not enough room to expand and hide in after porking out on *samgyupsal.*

I could never find hairstyles that fit me when I was younger. My problem was that I only had white women's hair for models. I liked the models' hairstyles, but they never looked the same on me. My hair texture was different. The first perm I ever got was a disaster. I seriously contemplated hiding out in my room for a few months until it grew out.

One of my classmates brought a friend of hers to school one day, who attended another junior high in a nearby suburb. The visitor was Asian. She had the coolest—and only—hairstyle I had ever seen on an Asian. Her hair was a little longer than shoulder length and was curly. Loose curls. She was wearing a bandana in it as a headband. I thought she was beautiful. My classmates agreed. Until then, I didn't think people thought Asians were attractive.

I went to the salon with a picture of her in my mind. I sat patiently while each strand was rolled carefully. I couldn't wait to see those rich curls—on my head. The stylist kept checking the rollers to see if they took. They had, but she decided to leave them in for an extra period of time because in her experience, hair like mine didn't hold a curl well. I wasn't sure she had too many other Asian clients in suburban Minnesota, but I didn't know if my hair would hold a curl either.

After waiting and imagining how my friends' reactions would be when they saw the transformation, it was time. As the hair stylist removed each roller, one curly lock fell after another. But as more and more came undone, they started to look very odd to me. They weren't the loose locks I had anticipated. When she had finished, I looked in the mirror—still hopeful. Within seconds, I was aghast. I think the hair stylist was a bit shocked, too.

The person staring back at me in the mirror wasn't me. It was a very strange-looking Korean girl with a very bad perm. The curls were poodle-tight and frizzy at the ends. My hair took to curls very well, after all.

I had a bad hair day for several months.

As a teenager, I was always fascinated by my friends who had big, blue eyes. Everyone was attracted to that feature. So was I.

Whenever I went to the restroom in high school, I always avoided my reflection in the mirror. It ruined the vision of myself in my head. I imagined that my eyes were bigger than they were. Looking in the mirror only brought me back to a reality I didn't want to face.

One year, colored mascara was all the rage. My fair-haired friends wore it and looked cool. It accented their blue eyes. I tried it out but discovered that because my eyelashes were black, it didn't show the color. I also had problems wearing mascara because of the shape of my eyes and lack of a double lid. By mid-day, it would rub off and form black circles under my eyes. I looked more like a football player than a magazine cover model.

Eye shadow was something that never sat well on my eyelids, either. Again, it was that lack of a double-lid. My smooth, oval lids smothered in sparkly, baby-blue shadow only made me look freakish.

A lot of women in Seoul have cosmetic surgery. Eye jobs are the most popular. In fact, I met some Korean Americans who came here specifically for that surgery because it's cheaper than in the States and the technique is better since it's become so commonplace.

The Korean word for it is *ssang-gopul*—double eyelid. The surgery makes women's eyes look larger and, therefore, more attractive. So they say. Of course, there are many Koreans who are born with larger eyes and double eyelids. Those not so fortunately endowed let cosmetic surgery do its magic. More men are having it done these days, as well.

When I did learn of it here, it never crossed my mind to have it done. The only thing I could think of was, "ew."

Like many other adoptees, I was usually the only Asian, the only minority, in my class at school. I did attend high school with about eight other adopted Koreans like myself, but I was only friends with one. The rest of us usually tried not to associate with one another. That Asian-phobia thing. It was like looking in a mirror.

My K-12 years were always filled with lots of friends. I got along with most people and was usually a part of some clique or another. I was friends with people in the classes below me and above me. I felt like I fit in.

That's not to say that I didn't have my share of bad experiences and rude remarks based on my appearance. I was teased, called racial slurs, discriminated against. But at the time, I didn't recognize it as such. Only after the fact. Only after I learned what racial discrimination was—to me.

Growing up in Minnesota, I was afforded a unique backdrop. Korean adoption has become almost a sort of norm. I didn't know any non-adopted Korean Americans growing up. I didn't know anyone who knew anything about Korean culture or the language. The concept of race and discrimination never seemed to apply to me.

And then I went to college.

Living in Korea is something I never thought I would do. When I was younger, I never had any interest in it. It wasn't a place I felt connected to or needed to see. I would've preferred to visit Spain and run with the bulls.

Now I sometimes forget where I am. I have become the norm. For the first time in my life, I am surrounded by Koreans. I can take it for granted. I forget where I am.

I am met by Korean faces every day as I go to and from work, riding the sardine-can subway. My co-workers are Korean. The *ajosshi* at the newspaper stand has a weather-beaten Korean face. The sleepy-eyed cashier at the 7-Eleven is Korean. The perky girls in their department-store uniforms who greet me while I shop are Korean.

So when I see a Caucasian foreigner, I do a double-take. They stand out. They seem large, their body language seems awkward, almost clumsy, they sound louder here. They are like an exaggeration of the norm. They no longer are the norm.

No longer the norm.

I went to college at Arizona State University. I wanted the anonymity of a larger college in a different state after feeling confined growing up in the tree-lined Minnesota suburbs. I wanted a new experience.

I worked part-time at a Japanese take-out restaurant as a cashier for a couple of months. It was the first time I was around so many Asians. Ironically, only one of them was Japanese. The others were Chinese, Filipino—and some of the cooks were Hispanic. None of them knew what to think of me. They were all Americans or held green cards. My first week there, the older Japanese lady who was one of the other cashiers asked me if I had a green card or working visa. I thought she was asking about my credit cards. I guess I was a little green.

We had a lot of regular customers and a few "celebrity" ones. When the guy who owned the Ford dealership in town, who was all over the TV with his bad commercials, came in with a vanload of people, we had to give him special attention. The first time I met him, he noticed I was new and asked where I was from. I told him. Minnesota. Eventually he got around to asking what my ethnicity was, to which I answered, Korean. He told me he sold Hyundais, too. I told him my father didn't buy foreign cars and went in back.

One customer was aghast that I knew nothing of Korean culture or the language and told me I'd better learn it because it was my heritage and that I was a shame to it. I didn't bother explaining my background. His opinion didn't matter to me. And at that time, neither did Korea.

I didn't befriend any of the Asians on campus, not that there were many. They seemed to segregate themselves from the rest of the mainstream, and I wanted to be part of the mainstream. I joined a sorority.

But I couldn't escape being Korean. I took a Race in the Media journalism course one year. It was an interesting class for me. It got me started thinking about race, discrimination and the bigger picture. Only I still didn't see how I fit into that picture. We had only four minorities in the class, including the teacher. Two African Americans (one was the professor), and two Asians, me and a Japanese American woman. One day our teacher posed a question directed at the minority students regarding growing up and race relations. But the question didn't fit my experiences, as she assumed my family was Korean. I also didn't feel comfortable being singled out like that to represent my race. So I replied, "I'm adopted. My family is white. I have no idea what you're talking about." I observed a very long moment of silence after that.

When I first ventured back to Seoul after accepting a job offer in October 1997, I wondered if my extended time here would leave me feeling more schizophrenic in terms of cultural identity. I wondered if I would feel more torn apart—more divided. I haven't.

I used to think I was pushing myself forward. When it felt like I was revisiting the same scenery with the same questions, I decided to stop reaching in front of me. I opened my eyes to what was around me.

The problem with my journey was right under my feet. It has not been the journey itself—as troubling and exasperating as it may seem at times. The real problem was with the premise. I picked the wrong road. I always have had a bad sense of direction.

When I stopped looking for the answers ahead of me, as if they were something to grasp, conquer and claim ownership to, I saw that the answers weren't what I was chasing. That road only led me to my own tail.

Had I seen another alternative, another path, I might have recognized that the trail I was following was what divided me. *That* in itself was the divider.

When we talk about cultural identity, we assume there is a split. And we waste our time trying to mend it. We talk about resolving a dichotomy, finding balance between two worlds, creating space for two cultures or building bridges. I don't think those things are achievable—or realistic. They are confining concepts rooted in dualism. Their resolutions lead you to separate, pick and choose or sort and categorize. What I'd really like to do is push *puree*.

The common question to ask ourselves is, *who am I?* But maybe we should ask ourselves what it is we want to know. Are the answers to that question more a matter of convenience than knowledge?

I have toggled back and forth between past and present, Korea and America, childhood and adulthood. I created the chasm. Easy, isn't it? Even easier would be to now draw a conclusion, offer some final words of wisdom and slap a bow on top. But I can't. I haven't reached that point, and I would only fall back into the two-dimensional trap if I did. I prefer to muddle in the mess.

To say that Korea has given me deeper insight into the *who* would be to tell people what they want to hear. To say that this experience has shorted out a few more wires would be to tell them what they expect. To come to a conclusion would be to state the obvious and make everyone's life easier, including my own.

So, we are back to the mess. I'd better go put on my wading boots.

Untitled

PETER SAVASTA AKA SHIN-HYUN TAE

I understand,
in small points of insight.
Your feelings delivered,
silently.

They were always there.
I never noticed
enough to
listen.

I believed my life started alone.
I resented you.
Separation burned your shadow
into my consciousness.

I neglected you,
Revoked your existence
as was my
legacy.

I was told to revere you,
a holy martyr.
I buried you instead,
with undelivered emotion.

But, now I understand.
What you've grieved,
on silent altars.
When no one would listen.

I feel your heart shatter.
Because I exist.
Yet I cannot console your
distant cries.

I understand
because you are human.
With tears already shed for myself,
I weep harder.

Your grief is
real,
as much as
my own.

I know you exist because I do.
You suffer because I have.
I suffer to know you have.
You love me, because I have love for you.

Even though we may never meet.
I have a silent understanding of you.
Not from your expressions,
words, or hopeful embraces.

I hear you, *amma.*
I know you.
And I know this,
by knowing myself.

A True Daughter

LEAH KIM SIECK

The shadow.

I was born from her body. But when I was so young—maybe four or five months old—she abandoned me. Like the night fog that covers the spring earth, her mother spirit faded away with the warming tendrils of the morning sun. When I awoke, I had no imprint of her on my conscious memory.

For the next twenty-five years, I lived with her shadow under my heart. It was a very quiet shadow. Only when I was eighteen, did I first allow the shadow to slip out so I could examine it and mourn.

I don't even know her name.

When I look in the mirror, what of her do I see?

When I was twenty-five, I went back to South Korea for the first time. The pain of disconnection walked with me every day. My mouth spoke only English and it stumbled over Korean. I was reborn as a twenty-five-year-old child, learning first individual words, then small sentences.

Good.

I am hungry.

I can't speak Korean.

I am American.

My friendships with Koreans frequently ran into jagged edges.

No, that was not my intention.

What is your intention?

I can't understand you.

Why do you do things this way?

Living in South Korea, my identity shifted uneasily between being a foreigner (and, thus, an outsider), a young woman ("helpless"), an American, a native English speaker (I was placed on a pedestal), and a Korean who can't speak Korean.

You are Korean. Why can't you speak Korean? (Meaning: how could you forget your Korean ways?)

Despite this constant disconcerting experience, I decided that whenever anyone asked me about myself, I would tell them that I am adopted. I would embrace this "stigma." I told taxi drivers— since they always asked. And *ajumas*, the ladies who run small sidewalk stores. Bus drivers too.

I'm not a ghost—I am not an unfortunate occurrence buried deep within the family history. I am not ashamed of my beginnings. I have remembered my roots and returned. Isn't this cause for celebration? Not castigation?

When they make me angry, I want to shame them, the men of Korea—like the taxi drivers who always curse me—for forgetting about me, for forgetting about the 200,000 adopted Korean people living around the world.

Oodi nada. Our country. Their attitude is: Everyone who left has forsaken us. Once you leave, the waters close around you and you are set adrift—to the outside world.

In contrast, I met a Korean woman in her early fifties. When she learned that I was adopted and that I was searching for my birth mother, she drew close to me and held my hand. She told me that she remembered that time, the 60's and 70's, and she understood my birth mother's predicament.

As a child, I would cup a seashell to my ear to hear the sounds of the sea echoing in that empty void. When I lived in South Korea, my unknown origins murmured to me. Indiscernible. Sometimes angrily. Or sadly weeping. Echoes of an emptied womb.

City Baby Hospital (Spring 1998)

I sit down with the hospital worker who remembered the hospital in the 1970s. Through an interpreter, he tells me at that time, the City Baby Hospital in Seoul took care of 400 to 500 abandoned babies every month. He is very kind and shows me the registration of an adopted Korean-Swedish woman who had just visited the hospital the day before. He tells me about a fur company who is running ads in a local magazine and who may publicize my information for me.

He takes me into a small room where the hospital records are kept. We look through the log book of all the orphans who were brought here in the 1970s. Every day, there are six to ten or more entries. All the babies, including me, arrived here nameless and are given names by the hospital staff. During that time, we all have the family name "Kim" since that was the name of the hospital director.

I brought my information that the agency sent to my parents. This is all I have with which to conduct the search:

Child's name: Kim Eun Sook   *Case No.: K-83*
Birthplace: Unknown   *Birthdate: 12-30-72*
Race: K   *Sex: F*
Admission: to original orphanage 1-8-73
Admission to Holt: 1-11-73
Adoption to the U.S.: 4-19-73
A worker in an outer-city-bus terminal at Shin sul dong, Dong dae moon gu, found her crying alone wrapped in coverlet at the terminal at 9:00 P.M. of 1/8/73 and referred to Dong dae moon police station.

I see in the logbook at the hospital that some babies have exact birth dates; perhaps they arrived with little notes tucked into their clothes declaring their real birthday. When we finally locate the entry about me, using the dates of entry and departure from the hospital, we realize that my birthday is estimated. It says "approximately one month old, birthday is 12-10-72."

This day that I have celebrated all my life is actually not really my true birthday. I feel like these little details that everyone uses to anchor their existence with, like birthdays or home towns, grow into big floating question marks. Can I live with question marks?

The hospital logbook lists my "place of origin" as Chung-ro police station. It is very far away from where my papers say that I was abandoned. Does that make sense? I thought that if I came here and looked in the records, they would answer my questions. Instead, they raised more.

Later, with a Korean friend, we sat down and reviewed all the facts that I know. I pulled out all the documents that I had collected while visiting various Korean governmental agencies. We constructed different scenarios: (1) I was found in the bus station. I went to two different police stations before the midnight curfew? Not possible. I would have to have been processed at both police stations. (2) I was found in the Chung-ro area. In which case the information I had could be false. Situation 3, 4, 5 . . . we go around and around, postulating everything, but we'll never know the truth.

When I left, I felt some desperation. Someone should photocopy that log book. It's the only record left that shows that we orphans existed in Korea. The paper trail of my pre-adoptive life in Korea is almost gone.

The adoption agencies and the Korean government agencies never thought we would come back to Korea asking questions about our origins. Now that adopted Koreans from the "first generation" are going back, things are slowly changing. But how different it would be if they had known that, twenty or thirty years later, we would want answers.

With nothing conclusive gained from that research, my friends helped me put myself in the public eye in order to search for my birth family. This was the culmination of two years of effort to get media coverage for my search. Right before I left Korea, I gave a dance performance, was interviewed in the national paper, and did a TV special about my life. Many friends and strangers helped me with the grueling process. In Korea, several women and families came forth, hoping I was their child, but our stories did not match.

Meeting the Birth Mothers (June 1998–present)

Their stories are overlapping waves.

"I was engaged to a military man. He liked many women. When I got pregnant, he left me. I gave birth to my daughter, but I had to leave home and work. I gave my baby to my aunt. When I came back for her, she said the baby was gone."

"I lived with a man for seven months. Our lives were very happy and I got pregnant. But while I was pregnant, he left. When I gave birth to my son in the hospital, my mother and the doctor arranged for my son to be adopted. I never got to hold him."

"I had two daughters and a son. The son was the youngest. Our family was very poor, so I had to leave home and go to work. One day, my husband took his two daughters to his oldest brother's house. They didn't want to care for them and made them sleep outside near the well. Later, a woman from that house took the oldest daughter to an orphanage. I don't know what happened to my youngest daughter."

When I look in their eyes, I see a deep black pain. It mirrors my own. Sometimes, I feel an anger—an irrational anger toward them—for abandoning me over and over. Words of rejection spill out, "I'm sorry, but our stories don't match. I'm not your daughter." It's my instinct to turn cold, turn angry. I hold back, keep my distance.

I also feel sad for this woman because I feel her willing me to be her child, her lost child. She is hoping to recover that child through meeting me. Often, she offers to be a "surrogate" birth mother. This is an unusual meeting—a daughter and a birth mother—even though we are unrelated. But I am not just a generic baby that disappeared through the veil of an impoverished time. I am now fully grown and a stranger. A person in my own right.

Throughout my search, my own unknown possibilities sometimes delighted me and sometimes depressed me.

I could have a twin sister. I could have an extended family of uncles and aunts. I could have many siblings. I could find my hometown. I could find my real birthday. I could find who I resemble. I could hear my mother's story—up to where our paths were divided. I could feel my mother's love again . . .

Or,

. . . I could not get along with my Korean family. I could feel disappointment that my mother and I are not alike. I could feel a deep anger toward her that I cannot overcome. I could be burdened by responsibilities toward her. I could want to run away. I could be smothered by her guilt for leaving me.

Vision I

June 1997. I am hiking up Kwanak mountain just as night is falling. Alone, I want to challenge my fear of being outside by myself, in the dark. Koreans are not afraid of the dark and feel that the mountains are an embracing presence. My cultural history has monsters and vampires that inhabit the night and my urban history has robbers and rapists who violate women in dark alleys.

After about 45 minutes, I make it all the way up to the top. Below me are the lights lacing along the Han River, all the colored neon lights of the shops in Seoul. There is only one other solitary soul enjoying the view. Behind me, the purple shadows of the other mountains invest the dark night air with majesty.

When it is time to go back home, I make my way along the top ridge. The air is rumbling and becomes muddy. Thunder breaks, and I hasten down. Through the trees lining the path, over the big table-like rocks. When fear overcomes me, I cling to a tree until I can gather up the courage to go on. At the foot of the mountain, I descend onto the path that winds through the trees. Walking through the shadows, my back starts to prickle and my fear balloons. I feel that a spirit is following me. Is it good or evil? When I finally emerge from the forest, back into the dull modern apartment complex where I live, I am granted a vision. In my mind's eye, I am in a deep forest at night. Far ahead of me is a tiny glowing blue-white bundle. When I approach it, I realize that it is myself, swaddled in a white cloth—glowing blue in the moonlight.

Myself, the adult, watches myself, the baby. The wondrous thing is that this baby is not the abandoned, needy child crying in a Seoul bus station that I have imagined before—myself in Korea in 1972. Rather, this glowing bundle is myself, the moment I came into this world. A spiritual, pure, whole being.

Vision II

Later that summer, I walk up the mountainside again. Not all the way to the peak, just halfway up, where there is a big flat rock that juts out on the side of the mountain. In the daytime, I can see the soft green forest that folds around the mountain. But now, it is night.

With a friend, I unpack my backpack. Fruits for ancestral offerings. Baby pictures of me before I was adopted. Candles and incense. I raise my hands above my head and then bow, kneeling down and touching my forehead to the ground. Three times.

I close my eyes and pray, "Mother, I remember you. I came back from America to meet you. I am your daughter. Come back to your daughter. I hope you are happy. I am very well. I love you."

I extend my hand out to her in the nighttime sky. I offer up my blue-white, glowing baby in my mind's eye. I offer up the stranger that I grew up to be. And the true daughter of Korea that I am becoming.

I invite her.

After a while, I feel her grasp my hand.

"I am here," she says.

I want to be the good daughter, remembering and honoring her.

In spirit, I can.

Mirror

REBEKAH M. SMITH

My daughter's eyes rest on the catalogue cover, move to the mirror, then back to the catalogue. Christie Yamaguchi's face is on the cover. Christie, wearing makeup and an American hairstyle—she is of course American. Her picture is an endorsement for crystal, china, and flatware. I notice the eye makeup, designed to enlarge the eye, shaded most at the outer corners. I've never used makeup myself. My daughter's eyes, which are not made up either, are confused. I think this is because she thinks Christie is beautiful and she thinks she herself is ugly. I hope I am observing in her a moment of deep, independent thought here, because I can't say much to help her.

I'm very sorry she thinks she is ugly. What if we had looked alike and she'd thought I was beautiful? Maybe she would have been convinced she was beautiful, but we never had a chance. She does think I am beautiful, but I was born in Richmond, Virginia, and she was born in Seoul, Korea. Or what if she had been raised among people who didn't look at her the way they did? At worst I saw a dislike for difference in their eyes. At best, curiosity or the on-alert with which people meet the unusual. What if a few of the faces she had heard called beautiful or pretty or nice had looked at all similar to hers? She'd be angry with me if I told her I think she doesn't feel attractive, so I won't. But look: she hides behind her hair, closes up behind her glasses, wears a face that says, "I am not asking you to look at me."

I know from my daughter's journal that she used to come home to visit and look in the mirror and find her face ugly. Lately, she writes, she drives back into her adult life two states away and sees an acceptable face again. (I don't apologize for reading her journal. If I have to resort to spying to be close to someone I love, I will do it.) And I confess, when I looked at my daughter's face during those difficult years I often felt dislike. After she stopped looking like a China doll, after she got older, I stopped loving her features. An overall roundness, fleshy jaw and lower cheeks, eyes not very large, small mouth. I never honestly thought she was pretty, though I hope I hid this from her. But what good is "pretty"? What good did it ever do a woman? It has been an easy ride with trickery at the end, cheap betrayal. My daughter is safer than I was.

It's also hard if you're one of those parents who goes through an "I hate you" stage. You think the drama in the constant fighting is killing you with exhaustion until you realize it's the guilt that kills. The only time I ever slapped her face was in a fight when she screamed at me, "You hate me!" I guess I was afraid at the time that it was true. She certainly comforted herself then with the thought that it was. It wasn't, of course, though she must have seen a lot of dislike in my eyes.

I can't tell her I don't like her foreignness, because that would offend her. But unless I do that, I can't tell her the reasons behind it, which are this: I want her to be mine. I love her. I hate anything that puts us apart. Even in the difficult years I was proud of her, wanted her to look like me so people would quit wondering how much my daughter she was and how much I was her mother. She has been so distant from me I have been terrified of losing her. If she'd been my own flesh and blood I could have hung on to that. You're connected that way, aren't you, even if they run off?

She can never know how much I love her. We are friends enough now, at least, to look at catalogues together. Maybe she doesn't want to be beautiful, or else she'd wear makeup. I suspect she just wants to be all right. The confusion in her eyes hurts me. I wish I could do something, or undo something. She is tough enough to be confused, though. I gave her that. And her eyes are demanding. That's good. If what she wrote is true, she has a mirror she has made for herself. Let it show her a face some day she can be always happy with. Her face makes me happy, I should add. It always did, really. Some day I hope she'll understand that, too.

Childhood Image

DEBORAH L. STAFFORD

My Han

KIMBERLY KYUNG HEE STOCK

*Caught in the passing crowd of dark heads, I wonder if my birth mother
is somewhere inside. Any moment I am sure the crowd will open up,
despite the heavy congestion of the Itaewon market. Maybe in the midst of
all those passing heads I will see a fortyish woman, her hair tightly fixed
in a bun, wearing a pink cotton shirt with little pearl buttons, gray
trousers, and a look in her eyes that almost betrays her past . . . a past
fraught with anguish and the secret pain of a long-lost daughter that she
hasn't seen in twenty-one years. She smiles to the outside world and full
cheeks redden as she laughs at a shared joke. Always she keeps one hopeful eye open looking for me.*

*And I too keep one eye on leather coin purses with painted Korean
women in hanboks that an older market vendor tries to sell me, and one
eye on that passing crowd. I fear I might miss my opportunity to see my
birth mother in person. Our eyes will meet and a look of feared recogni-
tion will pass between us. How could we not recognize each other? She
sees a reflection of herself twenty years past, and I see myself twenty years
in the future.*

*"Uhma-nim!" I cry and hold out my hands to embrace the woman
who breathed life into me . . . whose blood coursed through my body . . .
whom I must have dearly loved at one time in my life . . . who must have
loved me enough to keep me for eighteen months . . . who gave me up so
long ago. We embrace, tasting salty tears as we speak words of love, pain,
regret, and hope. Laughing wildly, I touch her cheek; noticing the lines
around her eyes, I recognize where I got my huge toothy smile. Stroking
my hair she tells me how she looked all her life for me. I forgive her—*

saying I understand the reasons. That finding her has finally connected all of the pieces of the puzzle of my life. She holds my hand to her heart and tells me how finding me has brought her the peace she's been longing for, for the last twenty years . . .

A flood of Koreans are pushing past one another on the sidewalk. Women wearing inch-thick white foundation and strappy black high heels. Men wearing trendy black T-shirts and matching Guess jeans. Hyundai, Daewoo, and Kia cars drive past me in flotilla formations that are supposed to resemble straight lanes. Mass chaos is all around us in Seoul, and this market vendor tries to straighten his cheap Korean souvenirs for foreigners like me.

I take a step back into the crowd of people and think to myself . . . "This is Korea . . . my birthplace . . . my motherland."

Going back to Korea I had no idea what to expect. Before my trip, Korea had always seemed like some distant land that didn't even exist on planet earth. Korea was always presented to me in the forms of bizarre stories that my Korean friends and acquaintances would tell me. They told me strange stories of arranged marriages, school children being beaten in school, and fierce family loyalty that could easily tear two lovers apart. These stories always seemed as if they came out of some Suzy Wong movie as I pieced the various bits together to form what I already thought I knew of Korea. I traveled with a group called a "Motherland Tour" for Korean adult adoptees. We were born in Korea, raised in America by Caucasian families, and speak perfect English. Except for our dark hair, almond eyes, and brown skin, someone could close her eyes and swear she was talking to a blonde-haired, blue-eyed American who ate apple pie every Sunday.

We all were painfully too American, ignorant of the Korean side of us that everyone else seemed to notice upon meeting us. I was excited meeting this group of people that grew up like me. Although our lives brought us to different parts of the country, our similar beginnings made me want to immediately bond with them. I wanted to hug everyone with the last name "Smith" and "Johnson" when we met for the first time in the Wendy's at the Portland airport; ask them too personal questions like, "How did you feel being the only Asian person in your family?" "How did you feel wanting to be white for the greater part of your life . . . and just when did you finally look in the mirror and realize that you were Korean?" "Do you feel as confused and scared as I do about going back to Korea?" But those questions never came out, and instead they were left stuck somewhere between the melted cheese and my Wendy's hamburger.

I shook the hand of each of the twenty-five adults on my tour group, smiled a nice Midwestern grin, and said I was happy to meet them. I was happy to meet them! For the first time in my life, I truly felt that I belonged to a group of people—Korean looking . . . American sounding. It was the only time I didn't feel like some crooked picture hanging on a white wall as we took out our photo albums and compared families and more-than-likely white boyfriends. For the first time, all the pictures on the wall were crooked, and it was the white wall that was out of place.

And so I knew we all looked for her. We wanted to see our birth mothers standing on a street in Seoul.

Our tour shopped at different markets, toured museums, ancient shrines and temples. We ate bulgogi almost every meal, and we laughed at the people who were just learning to use chopsticks. We enjoyed comparing stories and discovering what common interests we shared. We complained about the shower shortage, eastern toilets where you have to squat. I couldn't help wondering what our lives would have been like if we had grown up in Korea and not in our privileged homes.

It was a muggy Monday morning as we boarded the bus and adjusted our name tags with both our Korean and English names. We were going to visit the orphanage where babies were initially held before they are placed in Korean foster homes.

As I entered the office I felt I was stepping back into time. The dark wood and poor lighting contrasted with the sunshine of where I had just been. We removed our leather sandals at the door, and a group of us made our way up the stairs where the babies were. What I saw shocked me.

The nursery was a cramped room with about ten babies—newborns to a year. Some were quietly sleeping in their cradles, their little fists holding up their necks. Some babies were being fed at the same time by one of the two nursery workers. The nursery workers were young women, no older than me, and had at least two babies in their arms. The women seemed overwhelmed with the babies as they desperately tried to spread their love and attention to these infants who were waiting for families. I noticed one small baby, who was obviously very ill, connected to some sort of respirator.

I pointed to one of the babies. He looked like he was three months old, and he was wearing a white T-shirt and diapers. He had cheeks that drooped down the side of his face, and his chin was red. The woman holding him nodded and held the baby out to me.

"What is his name?" She said a name I wanted to remember, but lost five seconds after she told me. He would be renamed "Robert" or "Mike." As I held the baby in my arms I knew what I must have been like twenty-one years ago when my birth mother made the decision to place me for adoption.

As I held the abandoned baby in the orphanage, I realized he will grow up with that same sense of uncertainty about his birth mother. I pressed the baby close to my neck, nestled his back with my palm, smelled his soft skin, and I whispered a hope that he would eventually forgive her and accept the mystery of his strange beginning. I couldn't utter the name of this baby, but I felt connected to his tiny heart and spirit. We were both castaways, destined to live between two worlds—Korea and America.

On the long bus ride back to the dormitory I thought of that precious baby. Remembering the way he felt in my tired arms, I sobbed. Other tour members were silent. We were all thinking of the babies—the chubby ones with full cheeks, the tiny five-pound baby on the respirator clinging to his meek beginning of a life. Finally, I wiped my eyes and uttered the words that we all wanted to scream from the top of Seoul Tower. "I just don't know how they can give them up! Those babies, they're so innocent!" Dark heads bobbed slowly in agreement.

"I keep thinking of something that I haven't been able to get out of my mind," I said, feeling a bit braver now with my feelings. "I wonder if I've seen her since I've been here." (I didn't have to explain who her was). "I could pass her on the street and I wouldn't even know it!"

The trip to the center with the babies was in the back of my mind for the next couple of days. It was difficult to sit through language and dance lessons designed to teach us about our culture when I could only try to sift through the bitterness of Korea. The same people who claimed they were so loyal to family and country could also easily give up their nation's babies to Europe and America. I tried to bite back my resentment as our bus headed up a steep hill. We were heading toward a "hospital" or "safe house" run by the Salvation Army. This safe house was in a secret location where dozens of single, pregnant girls were trying to hide their different stages of expectancy.

The first thing I noticed was the smell. Sorrow has a particular odor that travels up to your nostrils and forces you to notice its salty-stale combination. Our group was led down to the basement chapel and encouraged to take off our shoes by young twenty-something girls, wearing less makeup than was typical, and Salvation Army aprons. These are the lucky girls, I thought, and nodded at them as I passed. These girls just work here.

The chapel was small. I wondered how the straight, cafeteria tables were going to accommodate all of our group, plus the women we were supposed to meet. We sat on one end of the table, and I noticed they had bowls of Snickers bars and cans of soda out ready to greet us Americans. There were also delicate origami animals made of different colored plastic. Their splash of color contrasted with the white walls, white table cloths, and the downcast expressions on our faces. A door opened and the pregnant girls walked in and slowly took their seats opposite us. I was struck by how young these girls were. They should be at home studying for their high school finals and dreaming about their latest crushes. Instead, they were in a home waiting in secret to give birth to babies they will spend the rest of their lives wondering about. I learned many of their parents didn't know that they were in this home or weren't aware of their "trouble." This is how deep the sin and shame of being pregnant outside of marriage is in Korean society.

A pink-cheeked girl sat on the other side of me. Her shoulder-length hair was pulled back with a black barrette; she wore no make-up. She was wearing an over-sized pink T-shirt, and I could tell that she must have been about seven months pregnant. I could see the worry, fear, and shame on her face as she crinkled her nose and pursed her lips together. She handed me an orange origami swan. I fiddled with the swan in my sweaty palms.

She nodded at me, and I was left with the realization that four months of Korean were not enough to adequately say what I wanted to say to this girl. At that awkward moment I realized that we both must have been thinking the same thought, "What must this girl be thinking of me?"

I reached into the front pocket of my backpack and fished out a note that I had written with my Korean language teacher. I knew I was going to meet these women, and I wanted to tell them that, because I was an adoptee, I wanted to assure them they shouldn't worry about their babies. Life in America would be good for them, and they were going to families that would love and cherish them. Their babies would grow up and understand why they were given up. I was planning to read her the note, but I couldn't quite double her pain by forcing her to realize that her child, like me, would never speak Korean properly. I slid the note in Korean to her. As she read, I watched her face. She never allowed her face to change, but I noticed her eyes tightening a bit. Our entire group was at a loss as to what to say to these women. Days before we had seen ourselves as the abandoned babies in the Seoul office, and now we were seeing our birth mothers. Jennifer took out a picture of her family.

Jennifer was in her mid-thirties, married, and lived in upstate New York in a nice middle-class home. Her wallet-sized picture showed her smiling Korean face, with an attractive blonde man in a gray suit. They held their biological daughter and a Korean adopted child. This mixed family looked familiar to us as adoptees. Jennifer handed the pregnant women the photo and tried to explain this was her family. One woman, who was very close to her due date, eyed the picture. Her hands tightened; her head fell to her chest. She dropped the picture to the table and moaned a wail that hit us with force. Her friends grabbed her to try to comfort her.

We knew what had caused her tears. When she saw that picture she saw her child, which she desperately wanted to keep, in a family that didn't include her. When she saw us, she wanted us to know the sacrifice and anguish that our birth mothers felt for us. Birth mothers and adoptees cried with each other even though we couldn't express our feelings in a common language. We cried for ourselves, for each other, for our past and our selfishness. We adoptees had been foolish to believe earlier that our birth mothers had gotten rid of us because we were simply a nuisance to their future plans. In that moment at that Salvation Army hospital I realized that my birth mother must still cry in her weak moments when she wonders what must have happened to me.

That day in the basement chapel, questions were finally answered for me.

Confusion, anger and bitterness seemed to melt away from me as I watched those pregnant girls freely sob. I began to heal.

A couple of weeks later I was on my journey back to Omaha, Nebraska. I forced myself to open my eyes and fight off my exhaustion as the plane taxied to the gate. The Motherland trip was behind me, and I had the rest of the summer to grapple with what I had experienced.

I eased my way off the plane too tired to even say "thank you" to the flight attendants. I walked up the tunnel as I tried to adjust my body back to Nebraska time. I could feel the Midwestern humidity through the thin walls of the tunnel as it seeped through my body. I welcomed the discomfort. I turned the corner and entered the airport terminal. I glanced around and noticed an older couple wearing red Nebraska T-shirts excitedly hugging their grandchildren. I looked through the crowd.

Finally the sea of tank tops and jean shorts parted a bit, and I noticed my adoptive parents standing close together with smiles on their faces. My mom was there in her shoulder-length blond hair and Birkenstocks. My dad was there in his light blue shorts, matching collared shirt, and calf-length white socks. I quickened my pace to them.

"Mom! Dad!" I yelled with my arms in the air. I hugged my mom and noticed her Estée Lauder perfume. I hugged my dad and stood on my toes to reach him.

"Oh . . . it is so good to be home," I said. And I meant it. These were my parents. They didn't give birth to me and they can't tell you any stories about when I was an infant. But they can tell you about the time I sang a solo in a concert or when I fell out my dad's van. I grinned at them and felt good as I walked with them to the car.

I still think about my birth mother daily. I realize now I will always think about my birth mother. Chances are I never did pass her on the street in Seoul or bump into her at the Itaewon Market. Koreans have a word called han *that describes how I feel. The closest English translation for this word is "unrealized dreams." I know that finding my birth mother is my* han. *I want to hold her hand and whisper into her ear . . . words I've held in my heart waiting to be spoken from my lips.* "Uhma-nim, juh han teh Saeng myung uhl joo shyuh suh gam sa ham ne da. Kyung Hee ruhl gak gum shik saeng gak hae joo shi goo me soe ruhl ha sae yo." *Mother, thank you for giving me life. Think of your Kyung Hee and know I am happy and safe.*

Questions

VINCENT SUNG

A Mother's Tale

K. SOO SWAIN

I stand
in the rain
in
the
cold.
My fingers
chill
in the
water
rolling
down the
wrinkles of
my leather
coat.

Blood-
stained
eyes, I stare
with the ache
of generations
at the knot
of my
most
sacred
ground
trampled by
my own
feet.

With distance
others balk at the mad dance
of secrets
as my children sink
beyond my
best intentions
(double-sided
with ungrown adolescent
hopes to survive the emptiness
with the life inside me—
not mine.)

Good-bye

TODD HYUNG-RAE TARSELLI

It's taken me a long time
but I've said my good-byes
I had to do this
but I know it's a lie
How many times I've wondered
who and where you are
how many times I've cried
why are you so far?

I hope to smile
to be free one day
to live a life
which was taken away

I felt you left me
to a world I know not
each day I live
a life I forgot

Hopes and dreams
a bridge I've crossed
love and life
that I have lost

If I can ask
to help me live true
can you answer
who are you?

Isaiah 49:15

BROTHER TITUS

"In Him there was only yes."
In His Body there was only yes.

>   my body feels the seeking of hands,
>   human hands; the hands of God
>   disarming my resistance, with the
>   warmth of

An Invitation.

>   feel, look, smell, taste, hear
>   your Orphan's Wail,
>   clawing at your walls,
>   tearing from your very Being,
>   all defense, and with it
>   the swells and convulsions
>   of the Unreleased
>   have turned to rust the ancient fetters.

Undone.

From the inside out, a tender confrontation:
"You comforted yourself."
. . . those nights . . . those days . . .
. . . to survive . . . to cope . . . to live.
And now I turn my body (soul), unable to bear it.
Yet, thank God, truth has not fled as far and often
as I have.

The Truth.

"She wasn't there."
Reeling in the suddenness of its
simplicity and honesty.
As honest as the conch shell
sharing its color and beauty with
the sky, its clouds pink and pearl.
The ground of pine needles and twigs
is truly aglow, and the Morning Firs
are thankful for the gift of Gold
which alights upon their boughs.

The sky, the sun, the moon,
water cascading in an unknown fall,
the yellow of the poplar; they are saying,

"She should have been there.
. . . and yet, there are no shoulds."

All of creation weeps with me,
and embraces the same truth.
A mother belongs with her child.
Always. Forever.

"Behold your mother"

> With what pain did Christ give His mother to us?
> With what pain and sorrow did the Mother of God
> consent to this vile separation with "Let it be done
> unto me"?

> The contours and tone of my pain are defined
> and realized in this bitter scene
> beneath the Cross of Our Lord.
> The Cross through which the Living Presence of her Son,
> was rent and taken away from her.

> Dare I say I know this separation? No I cannot.
> Yet, I do say, that which I know is known.
> This sense of separation which in an imperfect world
> has been the bond to the mother I so yearn for.

Mother.

> Korea is a mother to me, unknown and yet,
> known in my depths, for this very reason
> she eludes my clutching fists.

> She is also the tender woman who loved
> my presence
> in her womb, in her arms, in her life.
> My heart knows her; my body knows her.
> And the "I" in me, senses that to "know" her,
> I must be shorn of all "knowing."

> It is in this darkness and powerlessness,
> that I cling to the Mother of God.
> For in her, I see the fruit of abandonment
> I see the glory of separation,
> the triumph of loneliness;

The Power of a Mother's Love.

A mother belongs with her child.
Always. Forever.
Mary knew this as she sagged disconsolate,
the noonday sun burning her eyes,
shattered with tears, spilling forth
from a desiccated heart.
Broken, beneath the Cross of her
Broken Son.

Beneath the cool earth lay her beloved.
The stone, a speechless monument to the separation
between the living and the dead.
For three days she dwelt in both worlds.
Before it sufficed to ponder things in her heart,
but this? No. Only tears.

"Woman," He asked her,
"why are you weeping? Who is it you are
looking for?"

The Resurrection of a Mother's Love.

Just as their separation contained all,
so now does their reunion,
embrace and touch us all;
we are filled with the Light of Life,
as I write these words, I am with her
the woman who loved me at birth.
Also the Woman who loved through her.
Because Jesus Christ is Risen, and
Now, Always, Forever . . .

I am a child of the Morning Calm.

Who Do I Resemble?

MARY LEE VANCE

Children are often asked who they resemble more—their mommy or their daddy? The simple fact that I had been adopted as a young child was explanation enough for me to understand why I did not look like my adoptive parents or their biological son. In addition, prior to leaving Korea I had contracted polio, resulting in needing to wear a full-length brace on my left leg for the rest of my life. Although I did not resemble anyone I knew, this observation did not concern me when I was young. As long as I didn't look in the mirror, I could pretend that I looked no different from the rest of my family or friends, with the exception of a nonbiological sister who had also been adopted from Korea. The two of us were raised in a predominantly white area in Wisconsin. My mother was a professional musician, and she often invited musicians from visiting symphonies and bands to visit us. Some of the musicians were Korean. That they had anything culturally in common with my sister and me was not immediately significant to me.

The popular commercial showed blondes bouncing, in slow motion, across a lush green field with huge smiles plastered on their faces. The commercial said, "Blondes have more fun!" Hardly ever seeing brunettes, much less black-haired women, on television, I didn't take long to become envious of people who had long blonde hair. One day, while baby-sitting, I noticed a blonde wig in the bathroom. Fascinated, I stared at the wig, transfixed at the idea of being able, for a short time, to experience what it might be like to be blonde. I finally grabbed the wig and quickly arranged it on my head. Instead of seeing a head full of beautiful blonde curls, the wig had taken on a brassy appearance when viewed in the mirror. My normally olive skin had taken on a distinct green that made me look quite sickly. The image in the mirror did not remotely resemble the beautiful models on television.

At a young age I learned that kids can be cruel in school. Since then I have realized that cruelty is learned from adults. There were those annoying kids who just had to say insensitive things like "chink," "hopalong," and other names poking at my looks, my limp, or whatever else struck their fancy. Despite this, I almost preferred them to the opposite extreme—being rendered invisible.

Well-meaning parents generally were the ones who made me invisible. As I would traverse an area, walking by a parent and young child, the child would invariably stop and stare at me. Sometimes the child would point at me and then ask rather loudly, "What happened to her?" At this point, the parent would usually jerk the innocent child away from my direction, urgently whispering to the child "not to stare." For some reason, these instances bothered me more than being called "gook," "freak," or other slur. At least in being insulted to my face, I was being acknowledged and not considered invisible.

On the other hand, the alternatives included being associated with the Jerry Lewis Telethon "poor me, I'm a crip" victim club, the Hollywood "freak" line-up, or the "closet dwellers." It was a hard choice determining whether to cast my lot with Frankenstein and Captain Hook, the pathetic victims in Jerry's world, or people in denial. Other than President Franklin D. Roosevelt, who had also had polio, there weren't too many people for me to physically identify with. And, in the case of FDR, he approved Executive Order 9066 authorizing the Secretary of War to evacuate Japanese Americans into internment camps. Talk about mixed messages.

When President Nixon went to Peking in 1972, it was an historic moment in American history, as well as mine. The top women's magazines had cover stories on how to look "oriental." Mandarin collars, dark braided hair and "slanted" eyes were suddenly in fashion. Makeup tips carefully described how to use dark pencils to outline the eyes and create "slants." I laughed privately at all the blondes trying to look "exotic." I had learned my lesson early. I looked awful as a blonde, and the blondes looked awful trying to look like me. I finally understood that I was born with the hair color that best matched my skin. It was not until years later that I would wonder why the models advertising the virtues of the "mysterious" Eastern culture were not of Asian descent.

In college, I became involved with the International Students Organization. I went to African American Uhuru potlucks, partied with the Chicano and Hispanic students, attended American Indian powwows and did just about everything except associate with Asian Americans. The few Asian Americans I met were either "real" Asian FOB's (fresh off the boat), straight from the East, or like me had been adopted at a fairly young age. However, unlike me, the adoptees I met seemed to not want anything to do with other Asians. They did not want attention brought to themselves, claiming that they were "Americans" and acted upset if anyone associated them with being Asian. For obvious reasons, we did not get along. I reminded them too much of what they were trying to racially avoid, and for some strange reason what I wanted in my life—being with people who resembled me.

I would marvel at what an oxymoron I was. On the one hand, I represented a race and gender associated with being "exotic." On the other hand, I had physical characteristics due to post-polio that belonged to a population considered asexual. Realizing that people were often confused about my racial background, I decided to have fun with my chameleon characteristics. I would wear a Mexican blouse one day, braiding my hair with bright ribbons. The next day I would wear a silk brocade blouse with a mandarin collar. On another day, I would wear a gauzy blouse with delicate East Indian embroidery. I derived pleasure in confusing people, watching them watch me, knowing they were trying to guess what I was.

While completing my masters' degree, I saw an advertisement for an academic advisor/Asian American student liaison position at Michigan State University. I applied for the position, naively thinking I was of Asian origin and had a good chance for the position. Not until I was contacted for an interview did I begin getting nervous. I had learned that two of the people on the search committee had Asian names. For the first time, I was aware of possibly not being "Asian" enough. Until this moment, I had never thought anyone would question my ethnicity. I read anything I could about Asians in preparation for my interview. It was not until a year later, after I had been hired, that it would dawn on me that the resources I had read had all been written by non-Asians.

While I have long accepted the fact that I don't physically resemble my adoptive parents, I appreciate the fact that my resemblance to other people in this world has been so rewarding. Had I not been adopted by pragmatic non-Asians, I wonder if I would have understood the value of being so widely accepted. Whereas my official papers say I am a Korean, I have through the years humored people who thought I resembled them. For this reason, I always thought it was amusing that teenagers flocked to California to "find themselves" during the 1970s. To me, you are who you are, wherever you are. It was beyond my comprehension that I would learn more about myself by going to California. You could say my adoptive parents raised me well. I never had reason to question the fact that I belonged where I was.

Help Me to Never Forget

TINA WEBB AKA KIM SUNG HYUN

When I arrived in America at age six, I was severely malnourished. I ate nonstop, consuming everything I could find to eat. My insatiable hunger drove me to comb the grass in the backyard for clover. My favorite was light green with its sour flavor. This reflects my battle with hunger during my early adoptive years. I never want to forget my "starving roots."

Sour is light
Bitter is dark
What does this mean
I'm talking about green

Pine needles are light and dark
Clovers have bite and mark
So pluck away freely
Oh, there is plenty

Morning and night
Plagued by hunger fight
So where is my sour
I keep eating every hour

Ma, Ma I didn't know
You didn't say no, no
So I gobbled up the wild red
How will the birds be fed

Poison or not
Fresh or rot
It doesn't matter
I won't be any fatter

Hungry Jack
Give me any stack
You ain't no competition
I say this with exclamation!

Four square
That ain't rare
Plus raw and raw
Which no one saw

No time to cook
Forget about the book
It's the nitty gritty
Just a bare necessity

Why throw the rice
Give it to the lice
No bowl, no milk
Not even soy silk

Seoul, you are my kin
Ethiopia, I want to win
Help me to never forget
So I can repay my debt

Native "Korean" American

Or, How a Korean Adoptee Searched for an Identity She Could Call Her Own

LOEY WERKING WELLS

Throughout my bones, though perhaps not by blood, I am a true westerner. Molded and shaped by the towns, accents and attitudes of the American west. From the moment I landed in San Francisco in 1969 at age two, I have become part of the human landscape of western America.

It was funny growing up the only Asian who spoke fluent English in my school or town. Although I was not part of the recent immigrant community and felt very much at home with my friends and family, I knew by my looks alone, and my status as a Korean adoptee, I was not really the WASP I was being brought up to be. However, in many ways over many years, I've sought to embrace a culture or an identity that would provide me with a proper fit. A place where I was supposed to look different but where it was also assumed that I was all-American.

I began to identify with Native Americans, and a cultural fascination was born. Like the baby swan who had found the ducks because they were the only birds in the pond, following them around looking for a place where she belonged, I too studied, followed and embraced some parts of the Native cultures around me, whether they wanted me to or not, in hopes of finding parts of myself.

Looking for Culture

I was raised in a pretty "white bread" family. Although we never ate Wonder bread for our meals, my family was very conventional in many small-town American ways. We celebrated all the Christian holidays with much enthusiasm for the material goodies and a general nod to the goodness of the message; watched our share of prime-time TV (I learned most about Korea from *M*A*S*H*) and even did the "hustle." My parents adopted another child shortly after they "got" me and then gave birth to their last kid, which left them busy, tired and probably very stressed. There was not much time for researching Korean holidays, learning to prepare Korean foods or finding Korean stories to read at bedtime. There was absolutely no money for trips to an area with Korean culture, like Washington, D.C., Seattle, or even Korea for that matter.

All I had of Korea was an ancient box of terrible tasting candy and a horribly outdated book from the Korean Chamber of Commerce. That, with the handful of pictures from my arrival, was my ethnic heritage. This was before international adoptions were common, and very little information was given to adoptive parents about keeping parts of the adopted child's homeland alive.

To be fair to my folks, as I got older I really didn't care much about Korea. I didn't even want to be Korean, but I knew I was "different"—I still wanted some culture. After my Mom took us to see *Fiddler on the Roof,* I thought I wanted to be Jewish and took to wearing a scarf around my head and singing "Tradition" to the cats. Such was the angst of teenage years mixed with finding a cultural identity.

The Wild West

Western Colorado, Montana, California and Oregon have been my home. In the tiny towns and university communities where I was raised and where I went to school, I have found friends, intellectual pursuits and even love. But no Koreans. There were no play groups for adopted children and their families; no Internet to go on-line and meet people in Cyberland; no restaurants that served *pad thai*, let alone *kimchee*; and no kids who looked like me. In Montana you were either white or other. The American concept of a melting pot was utterly foreign. You couldn't even say there was a racial or cultural salad bowl, there were so few people to mix up with the white Anglo Montanans. Even being Jewish was considered far out, and the few Asians there provided some "interesting garnish" to the platter of ethnic sameness.

In Missoula, Montana, I discovered the world of Native Americans. Until that time I had had little exposure to the Native peoples whose land we had filled up and built mini-malls on. But at the university there were classes in Native American studies, a few powwows and some students whom I befriended while working on campus.

One Yellow Indian

So there I was in Missoula, learning about the world, and finally able to "discover" a world so new to me. I did not want to become Native American, yet I felt that I could be a quiet addition to whatever tribal life existed in Missoula by reading, watching and talking to others. I was in a cultural free-trade zone. My skin and eyes gave me an invisible visa, where I felt I could enter any world and go unnoticed, undetected.

After leaving Montana, I went to Los Angeles for two years. Finally I ended up in Portland, Oregon, where I have made my most recent efforts in my cultural search. I decided to go to law school in order to help fight for lands taken from the tribes, to protect religious practices that were becoming threatened and encourage tribal development and sovereignty. Although I had aged and grown less needy for tribal support, (could it have been because I had finally made some friends who looked like me and were like me?), I felt that my Asian appearance provided a mark of credibility and protection when working with Native American clients.

If I was ever asked what tribe I came from—and I was frequently asked that—I would reply "the Korean one." Having a name like Werking Wells, coming from Montana and studying Federal Indian Law, not being white, and not looking very Korean either put me in a position where I felt I could have been from anywhere.

Was it bad to embrace another's culture? Was I appropriating from the tribes a painful and proud past that should not be up for sale to the highest bidder? I don't know. Although I never consciously passed myself off as anything but Korean, was my desperate search for some identity—whether that of the ducks or of the swans—hurting both peoples? I suppose I can excuse myself and say that I am passionate about Native American rights, arts and history, that it was the only alternative world available to me in the situation in which I found myself. But maybe it is better to have no cultural identity at all, to be a polyglot of races, languages and religions, a member of the world community, than to reinforce existing divisions of race, language and religion.

She Will Mark "Other"

In 1997, at the age of thirty, I gave birth to my first child. A daughter who looked "just like me." She didn't look anything but half Asian and half white, which is what she is. After thirty years of not caring about learning who I was, or where I came from, or who was the mother who gave me up, I came slamming face to face with myself and all the Koreanness that is in me. My daughter is a beautiful mix of many worlds, and we know that she is so much more than the races of her parents. I know that people will look at her and know that she is not white—it's pretty obvious, and who would want to deny it?

But I want to provide her with much more of a foundation of who she is than I ever had. I want to take her to Korea, let her go to language immersion schools, and I never want her to be the only Asian in her class for twelve years. I want her to know that her mother looks different because she came from a land far away, a land rich with history, language and culture. So when she marks "other" for race on her census form, opens gifts from loving grandparents who celebrate all the Anglo-American holidays, and visits foreign countries, if just for a day at a cultural fair, I hope she never has to search as far and wide as I have for what may be very close to home.

Small Child Crying

BENJAMIN K. WIDRICK

Small child crying
Four walls so confining
An orphanage where hope had gone
Children dying of a broken heart

Small boy who looks a lot like me
Don't lose hope for God does see
A man and wife praying
That you will come and be their child this day

Small child smiling
As laughter echoes through the house
A new life you've been reborn
The Father's blessed the tears that you've cried

Children aren't meant to be broke
They're meant to be held in our arms
Father have mercy
For all the children who cry tonight

Still of a Performance

E. HWALAN SHUB

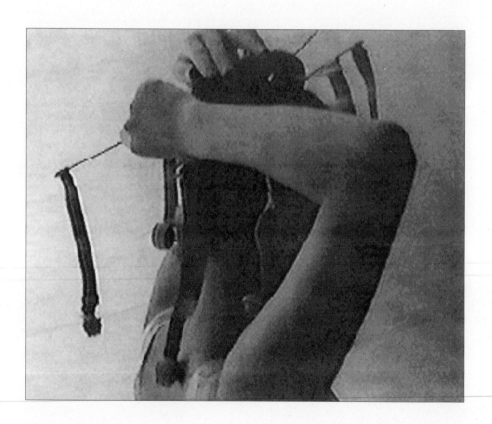

Returning . . .

WHITNEY TAE-JIN NING

As I watched the schoolgirls in their uniforms huddled around street vendors with their steaming offerings, I wished I had given into *umma's* persistence. Although my *umma* insisted that I wear several more layers, as well as her own bright yellow down jacket, I convinced her, and myself, I would be fine. I believed my growing up skiing down the Rocky Mountains of Colorado and scraping ice from my car before heading to school made me a winter expert. Besides, I didn't want to stand out any more than necessary. Seoul, a huge cosmopolitan city, largely abides by the chic, form-fitting clothes and sophisticated colors of black, gray and brown—certainly not frumpy bright yellow. I already felt like a "country chicken" in my baggy clothes and makeup-free face framed by long straight hair. None of that mattered, even how I walked gave away my secrets.

Despite the piercing frigid city air, I walked slowly among the soaring skyscrapers and the sea of Asian faces. I wandered aimlessly, with all of my senses in keen focus, excited, nervous and scared. I doubted I would ever feel comfortable in this immense city. Although this was my third trip to Korea since my adoption, the previous trips had been briefer and with my family members. Now I stood alone amid the cacophonic blare of the traffic and the ceaseless crowd in this cool city of Seoul. This half-day excursion, only "day two" of eight months of "getting to know my roots," left me exhausted and overwhelmed.

Soon I was in classes with students from all over the globe. Attempting to correlate faces with their unique names, to digest the bombardment of information on Korea's extensive history, to understand the modern sociological issues, and to conjugate verbs in *Hangul*, all seemed daunting. However, I survived. Within two months I too pushed and groped my way into crammed subways, and I knew where to find some of the best affordable Korean meals, the trendy nightclubs, a chic salon to update my hairstyle and even decent pasta and bagel shops. Four months later, I was seeing the country through the windows of trains, visiting every corner of the peninsula. During the sixth month, I hopped on an airplane to explore nearby nations. By the end of the eight months, I wanted nothing more than to extend my stay. I bid tearful good-byes to amazing friends, an endearing nation and of course my family—no longer my "Korean" family or "birth" family, but simply "my family."

I embraced the country. With all of its greatness and wonder—as well its rude, gruff, annoying inefficiencies and what I deemed outmoded traditions. In those short eight months, I began to comprehend this nation with its painful yet, at times, graceful transitions of defining itself. In doing so, I felt my search for "how to fuse my two beginnings and cultures," and to define "who I am" didn't seem so daunting. I did not have perfect answers to my previous questions or dilemmas, yet I no longer felt in need of clearly defined resolutions.

Somehow, in the midst of this frantic absorption and adventure, I began to feel more grounded within myself and with my newly cultivated understanding and love for my birth country. Despite all of my Americanization and the obvious differences, I felt incredibly proud to claim myself a part of this rich Korean fabric. The experience enriched me more than I had ever hoped, and it was uniquely mine.

However, uncertain and challenging moments marked this journey. Perhaps it is precisely these memories that I reflect on the most, and that subsequently have left such a lasting imprint.

Halfway through the semester, I had to give an autobio-
graphical presentation in the sociology class about Korean
immigration to the United States. The students before me told
stories of their parents immigrating under difficult circumstances, the challenges of the first years of adjustment and the
generational and cultural clashes between their parents and
themselves. Several also spoke of being forced to attend Yonsei
University by parents who were disheartened with their children's rejection of their Korean mother tongue and culture.
There were knowing chuckles from the empathetic audience.
I, on the other hand, could not fathom why they would push
away everything that I so willingly welcomed.

When my turn came, I went to the podium and began to
paint my blissful early childhood in a *shi-gor* of Korea. Then I
came to the point of my father's death, several years of dire
poverty, and finally how I came to be a "hyphenated" Korean—
just like them, yet not entirely like them. No, I didn't immigrate
with my entire family . . . only a part of my family. I left behind
my *umma* and *unni* and went with my younger sister to a whole
new family. Without warning, in front of the entire class, I
began to cry. I tried to stop the tears, yet they had a powerful
will of their own. I had told my story countless times before.
Why was I crying at that moment? Why now? Why here?
Although impeded by tears, somehow I stumbled through the
rest of my presentation. And finally, I concluded—"No, I had
not been forced to study at Yonsei. I have dreamt of it ever
since I was a young teenager and have craved to re-learn *Han-gul*,
hungered to be with my family, and longed to be just submersed
in everything Korean." By the end, I looked up and saw most of
my classmates wiping away tears from their eyes.

Mixed emotions . . . *embarrassment* for those uncompromising
tears . . . *anger* for my inability to control the flood . . . *relief*
from having released what I deemed my "secret" . . . *confusion*,
for where had all of my confidence and "togetherness" evapo-
rated? . . . *comfort* in seeing the tears in my classmates' eyes, and

most of all, *uncertainty*. I wondered how my classmates would now see me. No one ever questioned my "Koreanness" before, but would they now see me differently? I never tried to hide it—simply, no one ever asked me whether I had been adopted. Although, previously, I had hardly hesitated in sharing my adoption legacy, I felt self-conscious among nonadopted Korean Americans. Somehow I feared they would pity me or would not accept me as one of them. Perhaps this was subconscious, yet grounded in past experiences and projected fears.

Crying in front of the class actually pushed open the door. That day I realized that friendships built on unsaid truths and a sense of shame in how I came to be was not what I desired. Friends naturally had questions, yet my fear of rejection was indeed self-projected. They simply heard a story of a fellow student, a Korean American, a human being.

Being embraced into the Korean American fold was not about fitting into a "model." I realized there was no singular "model"—only the intersection of common threads of our inherently individual stories, layered and interwoven with each other in neither a linear nor a uniform formation. What became clear was that I had to confront my fears and wrestle with the meaning of acceptance—most important, the acceptance by *me* of *my* adoption story, despite the truth of being at times *too* unique. That day of those infamous tears marks when I returned to me.

The Surrounding Mystery

ROCHELLE M. SELBACH

I often wonder if I will see the face
That brought me life that mysterious day.
When I look back, I do not see my past.
Instead, I begin to ask myself questions.
I begin to see that I may not find the answers.
Although I know they are still lurking out there.
I go away and find others
Who are out to seek their past.
We can only hope to find the person
Who holds all the answers.
I start to think and perhaps
Those questions are meant to be left alone.
I continue my life, day by day
But the mystery still surrounds me.

Planted in the West

The Story of an American Girl

KAT TURNER

> Fear not, for I am with thee, I will bring
> thy seed from the East and gather thee from the West . . .
> – Isaiah 43:5

Dedicated to
Taylor and Chloe

For the first time I look into another face
And not only see resemblance to myself
But know that it is good
I believe some of what they got from me came from the generation before
Mama has had the privilege of calling them granddaughters
She knows there is another who would be proud also
I thank God they have been "mine" to keep

When I was pregnant, I began for the first time to allow myself to consider my own birth. I don't remember being told I was adopted; I've just always known. Dad was a Methodist pastor, and he and Mom adopted a total of four children. This was in addition to giving birth to five. Some would refer to them as my "adopted family," but as far as I was concerned, they were my family—period.

By the time I came along, Paul and Jo Ann Pfaltzgraff already had four children, two boys and two girls ranging in age from three to thirteen. Jo Ann had seen the Korean Children's Choir sing and had read a book entitled *Seed From the East,* by Bertha Holt. Jo Ann went into what Paul called "project persuasion." My future siblings offered such things as thirteen-year-old Phil taking a cut in allowance. Nita, who was eleven, would help take care of the baby, and seven-year-old Mark was going to play with the baby. Jo Ann gave Paul the book which described the suffering of these abandoned and orphaned children. After appealing to his conscience, she got his agreement to send for the application which "wouldn't commit them to adopt a child, she just wanted to see the application." Three-year-old Lynn proceeded to announce to anyone who would listen, "We're going to get a Korean child," which pretty much sealed my fate.

I came to America in July of 1962 at the age of one. Within several months there were six Korean children in the congregation of their church in Des Moines, Iowa. This included the three-year-old boy Mom and Dad adopted just four months after me!

Besides my rather obvious racial differences, there would be no secret made of my adoption. My picture graced the front page of the Sunday *Des Moines Register,* along with a story detailing the circumstances of my arrival. My mom and I appeared on WHO-TV, and Dad wrote a three-page piece for a Methodist publication. Thus my awareness of how I came to be a part of my family.

Ironically, the one who raised me wondered more about the one who birthed me than I did myself. Even now, I cannot remember how much of my curiosity crept into my thoughts during my pregnancy, or after my own child was born. I guess what matters is that the whole process of being able to give birth was ultimately the catalyst to opening a part of me I had not realized existed.

To say I had never given thought to where I came from would not be fully true. I do pride myself on being realistic and for the most part was never given to fantasies of what was, or what might have been. I always felt it was completely impossible to ever have knowledge of my biological parents. When a gentleman from the "home country" visited my parents while I was still very young, he seemed to think I had royal blood. (Does Korea have royalty?!) To this day I believe it is rather unrealistic to think I would ever be able to discover my "roots."

What I do remember, from earliest recollections told to me, is that I was abandoned at the city hall in Pusan, Korea. I was only one year old when I was adopted and always assumed I had been "given up" soon after birth. Later I learned I was put into a Catholic orphanage and transferred to the adoption agency. (Being raised Methodist, I like to tease my non-Protestant friends that I was once Catholic!) It seems that since the orphanage sent my parents a picture of me as an infant who had just come into their care, my birth mother probably actually kept me for several months.

As my baby grew inside me and I felt movement, I could finally acknowledge to myself that I, too, came into the world in this way. I actually began inside another human being. I always felt as much a part of my family as any of my other siblings, adopted or biological. I suppose my power of reasoning had never allowed me to consider my own conception or period of gestation. Now I wondered: what thoughts and feelings had I evoked in someone else for nine months and more?

As we head into the next millennium, America doesn't really offer many role models for a young Asian girl to relate to racially in the media. Thirty some years ago, there were even fewer. The few times I ever thought of a biological mother, the only picture I could imagine was of a stooped older woman wearing a pointed straw hat as she worked in a rice paddy. I always thought she was probably dead, because she would be so old.

Now I can imagine a human beginning, and it also causes me to confront my original misgivings. I am fairly certain I was the product of an American soldier in Korea as a result of the war. Could my mother have been young, even possibly in her teens, when she conceived me? Was this a young man also just at the beginning of his adult life? Did he know he was going to be a father? Those are questions that had never existed before. Reality can be harsh, but either way, the door had been opened, if even just a crack.

Until high school I was always the only Asian girl in my class and school. Usually I was the only Asian in the several towns where we lived. Being referred to as Chinese or Japanese wasn't meant to be a compliment as kids pulled their eyes back to mimic mine. As child number six in a family of nine kids, I could be as fairly aggressive about holding my position as any other middle child. But in public, my many insecurities caused me to be very shy. My dad was assigned to a new church about every five years, as is the custom in the Methodist system. I remember, in sixth grade, as my brother— who is part black and two years younger than myself—and I practically clung to each other on the playground when we first moved to Cedar Rapids. Until the novelty of our race, and that we were brother and sister, wore off, we searched each other out at recess as a source of refuge. Cedar Rapids ended up being my favorite childhood city. My shyness eventually gave way to my greater need of social acceptance, and I was part of what was considered a popular group in the three schools I attended there.

My junior year of high school found us in Cedar Falls, and my saving grace was a science teacher from our church, who let me chat with him while he monitored the lunchroom. I think I skipped eating the whole first week or so, to avoid being seen sitting alone by myself. A major difference at Cedar Falls High School was the presence of several other Korean adopted girls. It would seem that having someone else around who was Asian would make me feel better. Instead, from my perspective, another "Oriental" just brought more attention to the fact that I was like her and not like everyone else. This must have been a common insecurity, since none of us ever hung out together. By the end of my junior year I had come a long way. Trying out for cheerleading would have been unthinkable only months before. It was my first real test of courage where my self-image was concerned. It paid off, and I was selected.

I knew my appearance was no worse than average, and it seemed the lack of attention from the opposite sex was mostly attributed to my being Korean. It takes a brave soul to step out and be different. That was not the reality of young guys in Iowa during moonlight skates at the roller rink, let alone an actual date with someone from school. Why could I attract more than one star athlete from several other schools, but only friendship from those whom I saw on a daily basis?

A breakthrough happened for me the summer before my junior year of high school. At sixteen I was brave enough to take some initiative when I discovered that this great-looking guy, six years older and a cheerleader at Iowa State, was attracted to me. I must admit, I didn't mind being the object of a little envy of the girls who usually got the guy! This relationship made me realize I was as good as anyone, and it was partly others' insecurities, as well as my own, that had shaped a big part of who I was to this point.

Conflicting signals have plagued me as I struggle for independence, balanced with what is expected by others. More than once I have heard my mom say that the very nature of the strong will deep inside me is probably what kept me alive as a baby. I was severely malnourished, which was complicated by a case of diarrhea. The doctor marveled at my tolerance for pain as he diagnosed ear infections which I had not even whimpered about. I see in at least one of my daughters the beginnings of this same independent spirit. Did this start with me? Or did I too inherit it?

I was truly shocked a few years ago when I learned that the adopted Korean daughter of one of my neighbors was living my *déjà vu*. However, this wasn't Iowa in the 1970s, but progressive Minneapolis in the mid 1990s. I couldn't believe this generation of girls on the edge of a new millennium were not only faced with the same issues and insecurities, but to the same degree I had faced them almost twenty years before.

It has always been a bit uncomfortable checking that box in various applications which says "Asian." Am I in denial of my heritage? The answer is probably yes to some degree. If I need a defense, I would point out that my experiences have biased me in this direction. Although the reflection in the mirror appears Asian, American is all I have ever known. What is a realistic expectation of balance between biological and adoptive heritage?

I am finally realizing that I am the only one who can take control of my life. Insecurities aside, I am responsible for how far I go and what I become. I think of the parable in the Bible about planting seeds. I have been blessed to be planted in good, fertile soil, to be nurtured and looked after. Whatever weeds may come my way are unable to choke me, but rather cause me to grow stronger.

It is my hope that, like me, others will also know the blessing of a life transplanted from East to West; to be the beginning of a strong, rich heritage for those who come after.

Self-portrait

MELISSA McGOWAN

19 years ago, I arrived
confused
alone
foreign
a new country, new faces, new family
a new life

The United States
The melting pot—red, yellow, blue, green
brown, white, black
mixing and turning together to form a rainbow
the rainbow of humanity
a reflection of society, of life

But,
even in America,
land of hope, opportunity, equality—
so they say—
the colors remain separate, distinct
None can survive however, alone.
They are connected

Where am I?
divided in heart, soul, mind
I am Korean
I am American

not fully accepted by the Korean community
not wanting to assimilate completely into white society

It is the dual existence we all know about from past history and
experiences

Will I ever be fully accepted—
fully understood?

I am tired
no more words or energy to explain

Family trees weave in and out like the
veins in a hand
too many connections
too many ties

19 years later
I return

hoping,
waiting,
praying,
thinking

What will happen?
What can I expect?

happy
sad
confused
anxious
a multitude of feelings, emotions overflowing

All I can do now is wait
and wait

and live

Authors and Artists

ME-K. AHN is a writer and filmmaker. Her works, *living in half tones* and *undertow* have been screened at the Seoul Documentary Festival and the Toronto Film Festival. She is working on a novel to be made into a feature-length film.

JONATHON KIM HYO SUNG BIDOL is a writer, activist and teacher living in New York City. He is a co-founder of the Korea Exposure & Education Program (KEEP) and travels to Korea frequently.

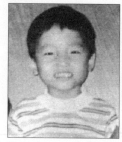 

THOMAS PARK CLEMENT is President and CEO of Mectra Laboratories, Inc., which manufactures medical equipment. He is also Director of Advanced Medical Technology Transfer for the Eugene Bell Foundation. Thomas is involved in humanitarian missions to the DPRK (North Korea), focusing efforts on famine, tuberculosis and the advancement of surgery.

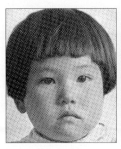

SUSAN SOON-KEUM COX lives in Eugene, Ore., where she has been an adoption professional for over twenty years. In 1993 she represented the adoptee perspective at the Hague Conference on Private International Law in the Netherlands. Susan came full circle in her adoption journey when she was reunited with her Korean birth family.

KEVIN DRAKE is a toxicologist who lives in Memphis, Tenn. Kevin is the proud father of two children.

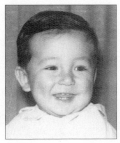

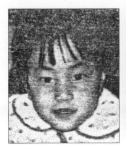

LISA DuFORE was adopted at four. She grew up in Lockport, N.Y., with her parents, sister (also adopted from Korea) and three brothers. Lisa is an artist who owns a custom picture framing business in Oswego, N.Y., where she resides with her husband and two children. She says, "My artwork reflects an ongoing desire to make a connection with my Korean heritage."

DOTTIE ENRICO is a professional journalist. Her work has appeared in *Glamour, USA TODAY, TV Guide, Interview* and dozens of other publications. She lives in New York City with her husband, Greg Dankert, and their daughter, Eleanor Jee Yoon Dankert.

INGRID B. FABER recently received her master of fine arts degree from Indiana University. As a first-generation Korean American, she feels it is important to express her feelings of identity through her art. Ingrid says, "I constantly struggle to learn more about who I am and where I stand in our society."

MARK FERMI, an engineer, resides in Belleville, N.J. He was adopted at age four in December 1974.

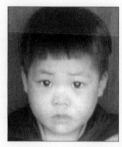 

SUNG JIN HALL lives in Bellingham, Wash., where she is finishing her master's degree in English at Western Washington University. Sung Jin will be moving to a bigger city soon, where she says she "hopes to find a diversity of elephants."

KATE HERSHISER PARK KUM YOUNG was adopted in 1976 and grew up in Detroit. In 1997 she spent a year in Seoul studying language, culture and traditional arts. Kate performed in Seoul at the Space for Shadows Exhibition in 1997, and co-directed and co-authored "Just a Moment" performance/art in 1998.

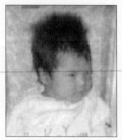 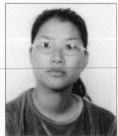

KARA JONES earned a bachelor of fine arts and MFA degrees in fiber arts as well as a fashion design degree from Parsons School of Design. Her desire is to become a successful fiber/fashion design artist.

TONYA KEITH was adopted in September 1972 and lives in Memphis, Tenn., with her husband, Rick. She is a risk analyst working toward her graduate degree. Tonya and Rick are adopting their first child from Korea.

AMY MEE-RAN DORIN KOBUS and her husband, Robert, live in Portland, Ore., where she is a counseling psychologist. Amy says she is "proud to be a Holt adoptee!"

JESSICA KOSCHER, director of a juvenile delinquency prevention program, lives in Elkhart, Ind. Jessica recently traveled to Romania with her family, where they adopted a ten-year-old named Robert.

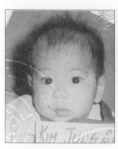

TODD D. KWAPISZ was raised in Michigan, then migrated to the Pacific Northwest, where he received a bachelor of science in sociology from the University of Oregon. Todd is director of Holt Heritage Camps, has been back to Korea and has visited orphanages in India. He and his wife, Amy, live in Eugene, Ore.

KAREN LAIRAMORE PETTY is a graphic designer. who lives with her husband and two children in Indiana.

MIHEE-NATHALIE LEMOINE describes herself as a "gemini-monkey Korean-born, French-speaking, Belgian adoptee." She is a multimedia artist, filmmaker, painter and activist based in Seoul since 1993.

JOY KIM LIEBERTHAL, aka Song Eun-hee, was six when she was adopted in 1976. She is a social worker and public policy analyst for the Evan B. Donaldson Adoption Institute and is a board member and mentorship supervisor of *also-known-as,* inc.

KIM MAHER was adopted from Korea in 1956. She is married, with one biological son and two adopted daughters. Kim wrote the words to her high school's alma mater, and her poetry has been published in books, anthologies and newsletters.

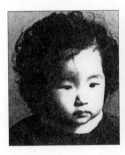 

HOLLEE McGINNIS was adopted at three and grew up in Westchester, N.Y. She graduated cum laude from Mount Holyoke College, where she completed an independent study on Korean adopted women and identity. In 1996 she founded *also-known-as,* inc., for adult intercountry adoptees, and has been reunited with her birth family. She is a project manager and website developer in New York City.

MELISSA McGOWAN graduated from Wesleyan University, where she was an active leader in the Asian American/Pacific Islander community. She lives in Boston, where she works for a non-profit human relations organization. Melissa has participated in Holt's Adoptee International Study Program in Korea and Holt Heritage camps.

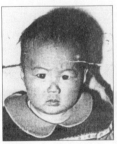 

JIM MILROY was born in January 1960 in Seoul, Korea, and was adopted the following November. He resides in Omaha, Neb., with his wife, Cheryl, and twin daughters, Ann and Jin.

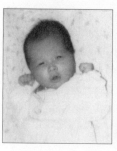

KELLY NEFF is a senior at DePaul University in Chicago majoring in English and history. Kelly plans to attend law school, then to pursue a career in public interest law.

MEA HAN NELSON-WANG was adopted at ten and raised in Tucson, Ariz. She is vice-president and treasurer of *also-known-as,* inc. Mea received her bachelor of arts in psychology from New Jersey City University. She works in New York City and resides in Weehawken, N.J., with her husband, Henry, and dog, Ivry.

WHITNEY TAE-JIN NING has spent almost equal halves of her life in Korea and the United States. Adopted when she was eleven with her younger sister, Whitney grew up in Colorado. She graduated from Colorado College, is the associate editor of *Chosen Child: International Adoption Magazine* and is pursuing a graduate degree in American culture studies.

JANE OWEN lives in Memphis, Tenn. A professional nurse, she runs marathons, loves the same husband of twenty-four years, and has three wonderful children and four beautiful grandchildren. Jane says that every day she "thanks the Lord Jesus for such a wonderful, blessed life!"

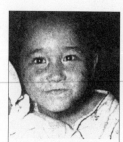

GREG PYLE graduated from the University of Oregon, where he was the first graduate of the newly established ethnic studies program.

JO RANKIN co-founded the Association of Korean Adoptees (AKA) in 1994 and co-edited *Seeds from a Silent Tree: An Anthology by Korean Adoptees* in 1997.

MELINDA MATTHEWS ROSENTHAL lives in southern Florida with her husband, David, and their three children, Benjamin, Nicholas and Kim. Melinda was adopted through Holt International in 1961; Kim was adopted through Holt in 1998.

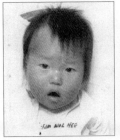

KARI RUTH lives and works in Seoul, but says America will always have her heart and be home. On culture and identity she says, "Definitions are trite. They belong in the dictionary. We do not."

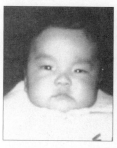

PETER SAVASTA, aka Shin-Hyun Tae, was born in Seoul in 1975 and adopted at six months. He resides in New York City and serves as president of *also-known-as,* inc., an adult intercountry adoptee organization.

ROCHELLE M. SELBACH was adopted in 1973 at five months and grew up in Grand Rapids, Mich. She attended Holt Heritage Camps, both as a camper and counselor, and participated in the 1992 Motherland Tour. Rochelle and her husband, Joe, live in Grand Rapids, where she teaches elementary school.

E. HWALAN SHUB is a visual and performing artist based in New York City, but is living in Seoul studying traditional Korean drumming and dance, including the Sol Changu. While there, she wrote, co-directed and produced "Re-Birth," an adult fairy tale performed with life-size puppets and original Korean music.

LEAH KIM SIECK (Kim Eun Sook) was adopted in 1973 at five months and grew up in Indianapolis. At Wesleyan University she wrote her English literature honors thesis on adopted Korean American identity. Leah taught English in Seoul through the Princeton-in-Asia program and performed dance/poetry pieces about being adopted. She lives in Indiana, where she is finishing a Master's in physiology and preparing for medical school.

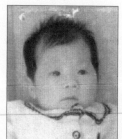

REBEKAH M. SMITH was adopted in 1961 and is a part-time college teacher and research scholar in classical studies. She lives in Chapel Hill, N.C., with her husband, Peter, and has two stepchildren.

DEBORAH L. STAFFORD (Kim Yung Hee) was adopted from Seoul in June 1958. She resides in Wisconsin and has three adult sons and one grandchild. Deborah is employed by Family Advocates and works with the handicapped. She is an artist who says she is often inspired through her interactions with children or nature.

KIMBERLY KYUNG HEE STOCK is a high school English teacher in a suburb near Boston. She traveled back to Korea with the Holt Motherland Tour in 1998. It is from this experience that she wrote the story in this anthology. Kimberly is helping to establish a group for Korean adoptees in Boston.

VINCENT SUNG is a visual artist/photographer living and working in New York City. Born in Korea, educated in Belgium, "big travels" finally made him an "Earth-oriented artist." He is now preparing a "book/film" project to be released in 2000.

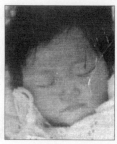

K. SOO SWAIN, aka Kelli Marie Swain, Soo Jin Nam, was born in 1973 and adopted from Seoul in 1974. She is a painter, art therapist and poet residing in New York City.

TODD HYUNG-RAE TARSELLI currently lives in Pennsylvania and hopes to return to Korea one day.

BROTHER TITUS was adopted from Korea in 1975. He is a monk at the Holy Transfiguration Monastery in Redwood Valley, Calif., where he lives according to the ancient monastic and spiritual tradition of the Christian East.

KAT TURNER was adopted at age one in July 1962 and was raised in Iowa. She has lived in San Antonio, Dallas and Atlanta, and now lives in Minneapolis. Kat says, "Living in these places has allowed me to interact and communicate with people from all walks of life." She has been the director of a small non-profit foundation with programs for inner-city and low-income children. Kat has two daughters, Taylor and Chloe.

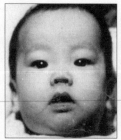

MARY LEE VANCE earned her doctorate at Michigan State University while working full time as an academic advisor and Asian Pacific American student liaison. She is an administrator at George Mason University in Fairfax, Va. Mary Lee loves living, working and eating in the Washington, D.C., area. She is particularly fond of the Korean restaurants that serve hot and spicy kimchee.

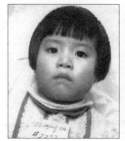 

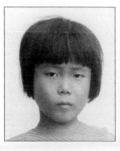 

TINA WEBB, aka Kim Sung Hyun, resides in Portland, Ore., with her spouse. She earned her associate degree in occupational therapy. One of her favorite poems is "The Road Not Taken," by Robert Frost.

LOEY WERKING WELLS lives in Portland, Ore., where she received her law degree in 1996. She works out of the home with her sole client, Dylan— her young daughter. Dylan and Loey's husband, Andy, keep her busy and sane.

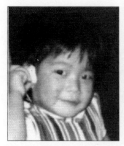 

BENJAMIN K. WIDRICK lives in Pensacola, Fla., with his wife, Meagan. He is studying multimedia and the fine arts.

Acknowledgments

Voices from Another Place was published as part of the International Gathering of the First Generation of Korean Adoptees in September 1999, in Washington, D.C. Selections were made by the Gathering planning committee and include the work of adoptees from Europe and the United States, and of adoptees who are now living in South Korea.

Voices from Another Place was touched by many people who helped bring it to life. Special appreciation to Michele Porter, who with her usual good nature and impeccable sense of organization, coordinated the details between authors, artists and everyone else involved in the publication of this book. Thanks to John Aeby, for designing the book jacket and providing thoughtful insights about the pages in between. I am also grateful to John Williams who understood the importance of bringing all these voices together.

I especially wish to acknowledge and thank all the authors and artists who contributed to this book. They did so without compensation, and this book would not have been possible without them.

Finally, my thanks for the support of Brian Boyd and Yeong & Yeong Book Company for bringing all of these efforts and voices together. A portion of the proceeds of the sale of *Voices from Another Place* will benefit the lives of children whose voices have yet to be heard.